RADIX READING for the TOEFL iBT®

BLUE LABEL

1

TABLE OF **CONTENTS**

INTRODUCTION

TOEFL®: Test of English as a Foreign Language

The TOEFL is a standardized test developed to assess English language proficiency in an academic setting. By achieving a high score on the TOEFL, you will demonstrate that your skills in English qualify you for admission to a college or university where English is used as the language of instruction. Academic institutions around the world will look at your performance on the TOEFL, so whether you are hoping to study in North America, Australia, Europe, or Asia, this test is the key to your future educational career.

TOEFL Today: TOEFL iBT

The TOEFL Internet-based test (iBT) is the version currently administered in secure testing centers worldwide. It tests reading, listening and writing proficiency, and speaking abilities.

Getting to Know the TOEFL iBT: Test Format

You will take all four sections of the test (Reading, Listening, Speaking, and Writing) on the same day. The duration of the entire test is about four hours.

Test Section	Description of Tasks	Timing
Reading	3–4 passages, each approximately 700 words 10 questions on each passage	54–72 minutes

Listening	• 3–4 lectures, each 3–5 minutes long
	  6 questions per lecture
	• 2–3 conversations, each around 3 minutes long
	  5 questions per conversation
		41–57 minutes

BREAK		10 minutes
Speaking	4 tasks • 1 independent task – speak about personal knowledge and experience • 3 integrated tasks – read-listen-speak / listen-speak	17 minutes
Writing	2 tasks • 1 independent task – write about personal knowledge and experience • 1 integrated task – read-listen-write	50 minutes

Score Scales

You will receive a score between 0 and 30 for each section of the test. Your total score is the sum of these four scores and will be between 0 and 120.

Registering for the TOEFL iBT

The most convenient way to register to take the TOEFL iBT is online by visiting the "Register for the TOEFL® Test" section of the TOEFL website (www.ets.org/toefl). Here, you can check current listings of testing centers and schedules. It is also possible to register for the test by phone and by mail. For more information, consult the TOEFL iBT Bulletin, which can be downloaded or ordered from the TOEFL website. It is free and features important information regarding the registration process.

GUIDE TO READING

Success in an English-speaking academic environment demands high-level reading comprehension skills. The Reading Section of the TOEFL iBT requires you to understand and analyze texts similar to those used at academic institutions across North America and throughout the world. Questions in the Reading Section are designed to test:

1. Your ability to identify important details in an academic text, including the meaning of selected vocabulary terms, the noun referred to by a pronoun or other reference word, the fundamental meaning of complex sentences, and facts relevant to the main idea of a passage
2. Your ability to draw inferences regarding implied information, the intent or attitude of the author, and the relationship between ideas in different parts of a passage
3. Your understanding of the organization of a passage, including how major points relate to the main idea and how an individual sentence is connected to the sentences around it

Reading Section Content: Types of Passages

The material you will see in the Reading Section will include texts typical of college-level textbooks used in introductory courses. Topics covered are quite varied, but no prior knowledge or expertise is required to understand the material. You will be able to answer all the questions using only the information contained in the passages.

Passages that appear in the Reading Section fall into three categories:
1. Exposition: a text that is factual in nature, with the primary purpose of providing an explanation of a topic
2. Argumentation: a text offering a specific point of view on an issue, with the primary purpose of persuading readers through the presentation of evidence
3. Historical/Biographical: a text providing an account of a historical event or the life of a notable individual

Types of Questions

The questions found in the Reading Section can be divided into 9 categories.

Question Type	Testing Point
Vocabulary	The meaning of a highlighted word or phrase, determined by context
Reference	The noun referred to by a pronoun or other reference word
Fact & Negative Fact	Important details presented in the passage / An idea that is not factually correct according to the passage
Sentence Simplification	The fundamental meaning of a complex sentence
Inference	Information that is implied, rather than directly stated, in the passage
Rhetorical Purpose	The author's purpose for including certain information in the passage
Insertion	The logical position at which to insert a given sentence into the passage
Prose Summary	The completion of a summary of the passage by choosing the most relevant and important information
Schematic Table	The correct categorization of information from the passage

Important Points to Keep in Mind

≫ Questions appear only after you have scrolled to the end of the passage. After they appear, you will be able to see the passage on the right side of the screen as you answer the questions on the left.

≫ Certain words and phrases in the passages will have a "Glossary Feature" associated with them. Clicking on these underlined words and phrases will produce a box containing a definition or explanation.

Tactics for the TOEFL iBT Reading Section

To strengthen your reading skills before taking the TOEFL iBT, it is essential to expose yourself frequently to written English. Focus should be placed on texts that are academic in nature, but it is also important to seek out material from diverse sources that cover a variety of topics.

During the test, remember to:

- write down brief notes about the organization, main idea, and key details of the passage
- pay attention to the flow of ideas in the passage and how they relate to one another
- think about the author's motivation for writing the passage and presenting certain information
- determine the key words of answer choices and locate them in the passage to help you identify the correct answer

HOW TO USE THIS BOOK

This book gives you instruction, practice, and strategies for performing well on the TOEFL iBT Reading Section. It will familiarize you with the appearance and format of the TOEFL iBT and help you prepare for the TOEFL test efficiently.

Each unit in the book corresponds to one of the nine question types in the Reading Section. Each unit consists of the following:
- An **Introduction** that provides basic information about the question type
- **Basic Drills** that offer short passages with 1–3 questions designed to familiarize you with specific question types
- **Reading Practice** that involves longer passages with 3–4 questions so that you can master skills for specific question types
- **iBT Practice** that includes long passages with 5–6 questions to help you experience and practice a variety of question types
- A **Vocabulary Review** that offers a variety of activities to help you increase your vocabulary knowledge

In addition, this book contains three **Actual Practice Tests** to help you measure your progress, and these appear after units 4, 6, and 9.

PART

Identifying Details

UNIT

Vocabulary

■ Vocabulary questions ask about the meaning of a word or phrase in the passage.

QUESTION TYPES

• The word [ ] in the passage is closest in meaning to

• The phrase [ ] in the passage is closest in meaning to

The human body prefers to stay at a temperature of about 37°C. That is the temperature at which the body feels most comfortable and works best. In certain circumstances, however, your body temperature may rise above 37°C. This can happen 5 during exercise or if it is hot. Your body responds to this increase in body temperature by sweating. It is a way of getting rid of unnecessary heat. Sweat is produced by sweat *glands that are distributed throughout the whole body. When the sweat glands release sweat, the drops come to the surface of the skin through very small holes known as pores. As sweat meets the air on the surface of the 10 skin, it starts to evaporate, or turn into a gas. When sweat undergoes evaporation, it has a cooling effect and lowers the body's temperature.

*gland: an organ of the body that produces a substance for various purposes

1 The phrase getting rid of in the passage is closest in meaning to

Ⓐ keeping   Ⓑ removing

Ⓒ changing   Ⓓ preventing

2 The word distributed in the passage is closest in meaning to

Ⓐ used   Ⓑ given

Ⓒ spread out   Ⓓ put together

3 The word undergoes in the passage is closest in meaning to

Ⓐ controls   Ⓑ becomes

Ⓒ produces   Ⓓ experiences

BASIC DRILLS 02

The term "diaspora" refers to a large number of people that have been forced to depart from their traditional homelands. The reasons for these large-scale population movements are varied. In some cases, diasporas form as a result of political incidents, when a government forces certain people to move. In other cases, populations move to avoid mistreatment or to escape violence in their home country. In any event, 5 members of a diaspora generally keep their cultural and religious traditions alive.

One of the largest diasporas in the world is the African diaspora. The forced movement of African people began in the sixteenth century with the Atlantic slave trade. Huge populations of African people were moved to Western countries like Brazil and the United States. As a result, African diaspora populations in North and South 10 America now number in the hundreds of millions. It is no surprise, then, that elements of African cultures, such as music, religion, and language, have had a major influence on the cultures of the Americas.

1 The phrase depart from in the passage is closest in meaning to

(A) leave   (B) set up
(C) give up   (D) destroy

2 The word incidents in the passage is closest in meaning to

(A) limits   (B) events
(C) conflicts   (D) changes

3 The word elements in the passage is closest in meaning to

(A) studies   (B) records
(C) parts   (D) traditions

Wombats

Wombats are bear-like mammals that live in forests and mountains throughout southeast Australia. The size of a full-grown wombat stretches to lengths of about one meter. Their body weights fall between 25 and 35 kilograms. They have small eyes 5 and ears and a large nose. Four short legs support their round bodies, which are covered with thick fur.

→ One interesting characteristic of wombats is their pouch. ■ Like kangaroos, female wombats have an external pouch for carrying their babies. ■ However, unlike kangaroos, wombats' pouches face backwards. ■ The reason for this unusual pouch 10 position is due to the fact that the wombat is an animal which builds underground tunnels. ■ Wombats make long tunnels to keep themselves cool during the heat of the day. Some of these tunnels extend for lengths of up to 20 meters. Wombats create these structures with the help of strong front legs and short claws. Obviously, if they had the same kind of forward-facing pouches as kangaroos, digging tunnels would 15 fill the pouches up with soil and threaten the babies held within. A rear-facing pouch, however, ensures that the baby wombats stay safe and clean.

1 The phrase stretches to in the passage is closest in meaning to
Ⓐ develops   Ⓑ varies
Ⓒ increases   Ⓓ reaches

2 The word external in the passage is closest in meaning to

(A) useful   (B) large

(C) outside   (D) special

3 Look at the four squares [■] that indicate where the following sentence could be added to the passage.

> For this reason, scientists believe that wombats and kangaroos may have the same ancestor.

Where would the sentence best fit?

4 In paragraph 2, why does the author mention that the wombat builds underground tunnels?

(A) To indicate how wombats reproduce

(B) To describe why wombats have strong front legs

(C) To explain the reason why the pouch faces backwards

(D) To show one of the similarities between wombats and kangaroos

Paragraph 2 is marked with an arrow [→].

🗗 **ORGANIZATION**

- Characteristics of wombats
  - bear-like _____ found in southeast Australia
  - covered in thick _____, with short legs and _____ bodies
- The unusual pouch
  - carry their babies in a pouch that faces _____
  - suitable for building _____ tunnels
  - thanks to the position of their pouch, baby wombats stay safe and clean within it

The Butterfly Effect

The butterfly effect is a concept that arose out of chaos theory. It explains how the smallest action can have huge impacts in another part of the world. It was discovered by Edward Lorenz, a mathematician and meteorologist. During one of his lectures, Lorenz first introduced his famous example of the theory, stating that "a butterfly flapping its wings in Brazil can produce a tornado in Texas."   5

Lorenz noted the phenomenon while inputting meteorological *variables into his computer to run a simulation. He wanted to run a second simulation on some of his data and compare it with the first. To save time, he started the second simulation from the middle, which, in effect, meant rounding variables from the original. These rounded numbers caused more and more errors to accumulate the longer the simulation   10 continued. Lorenz's findings indicated that just very small changes in air temperature or wind speed had considerable impacts on future weather patterns, and even climate change. This phenomenon is now called chaos. Chaotic systems are unpredictable systems that are greatly affected by small changes in a single variable.

The butterfly effect is not only unique to weather, however. In nature, it can   15 be found in the fields of chemistry, economics, ecology, and psychology. The phenomenon even operates within marketplaces, where an accumulation of seemingly meaningless events can lead to great economic growth or the bankruptcies of giant corporations.

variable: a mathematical quantity which can represent several different amounts

1   The word noted in the passage is closest in meaning to
   (A) wrote   (B) revised
   (C) noticed   (D) popularized

2 The word it in the passage refers to

   (A) tornado

   (B) his computer

   (C) phenomenon

   (D) second simulation

3 The word accumulate in the passage is closest in meaning to

   (A) grow   (B) separate

   (C) occur   (D) remain

4 According to the passage, which of the following is NOT true about the butterfly effect?

   (A) It was first found by Edward Lorenz.

   (B) It was discovered while comparing two meteorological simulations.

   (C) It shows how small changes can have big impacts in predictable systems.

   (D) It can be observed in a variety of fields from science to economics.

▣ SUMMARY

The butterfly effect is a phenomenon that was first discovered by Edward Lorenz. While running a _____ simulation, he noted how just very _____ changes in air temperature or wind speed had huge impacts on future weather patterns. This phenomenon is now called _____, with chaotic systems referring to _____ systems that are largely affected by small changes in a(n) _____ variable. Interestingly, this phenomenon is also found in other aspects of nature and human society.

30 St. Mary Axe

→ 30 St. Mary Axe is a famous glass-covered tower in London. It was built in 2003 on the site where the Baltic Exchange, a building which was bombed in 1992, used to stand. The building is home to offices of many companies such as the global insurance firm 5 Swiss Re. Its design has a strong frame with triangular panels on the outside and spacious circular floor plan on the inside. The 41 floors of the tower are round and larger in the middle than at the bottom. The building forms a point at the top and has been nicknamed the "Gherkin" because of its pickle-like shape. 10

→ The tower was planned as an environmentally-friendly building. The thicker middle section and continuous windows help to let air and sunlight into the building. There are gaps in each floor, with six pipes in each gap. The gaps pull air out of the building in the summer and pass heat from the sun into the building in the winter. During the day, sunlight gets deep inside the building, which reduces the need for 15 artificial light. Because of these features, 30 St. Mary Axe costs half of what a similar-sized building might cost to cool, heat, and light. The shape also makes wind flow around the building, rather than pushing it down to the street. This means the wind doesn't shake the building or bother people walking around the bottom. As one of the most recognizable buildings in the London skyline, 30 St. Mary Axe is also one of the 20 most innovative.

1 The word site in the passage is closest in meaning to

   Ⓐ view   Ⓑ location

   Ⓒ heritage   Ⓓ street

2   According to paragraph 1, which of the following is NOT true about 30 St. Mary Axe?

Ⓐ Its outer wall is covered with glass.

Ⓑ It is being used as a residential property.

Ⓒ It is thickest in the middle and thinnest at the top.

Ⓓ It got its nickname, "the Gherkin," from its appearance.

Paragraph 1 is marked with an arrow [➡].

3   The word features in the passage is closest in meaning to

Ⓐ highlights   Ⓑ accents

Ⓒ characteristics   Ⓓ advantages

4   According to paragraph 2, which of the following does NOT help 30 St. Mary Axe reduce its energy use?

Ⓐ The size of the middle section

Ⓑ The continuous windows

Ⓒ The gaps in each floor

Ⓓ The lighting control system

Paragraph 2 is marked with an arrow [➡].

ORGANIZATION

- 30 St. Mary Axe
  - built on the former site of the Baltic Exchange, in _____
  - used as an office building by many companies
- Exterior
  - has a frame of triangular panels
  - _____-like shape (larger in the _____ than at the bottom)
- Environmentally-friendly features
  - thicker middle section, continuous windows and _____ in each floor let more air and _____ into the building
  - uses less energy to cool, _____, and light

VOLUME　HELP　OK　NEXT

A New Style of Art: Impressionism

➡ French art in the mid-1800s followed several rules. Paintings were always done in studios, not outdoors. The subject of a painting, usually a person or group of people, was always placed in the center of the work. The details of the subject were painted very realistically, and dark colors were used for the background. But in the 1860s and '70s, a group of young artists decided to try something new. These painters – Renoir, Monet, Sisley, and Bazille – created the style known as Impressionism, which changed the art world forever.

➡ Impressionist artists painted from a new point of view. They left their studios and went out into nature to create their works. Instead of painting subjects in fine detail, they tried to capture their own individual idea, or impression, of the moment. In doing so, the painters tended to use quick, clear brushstrokes and bright colors. They were also very interested in how light was able to change the shadows and colors of their subjects. Monet, for example, was famous for painting the same scene at different times of day to show how changes in light affected its appearance.

➡ At first, Impressionist art was not accepted by the public. Many art critics thought the paintings looked incomplete and unclear. Soon, though, other artists began working in the Impressionist style. They liked it, for it allowed them to express their own unique vision of a subject and create a truly individual work. Impressionism eventually became very popular, and its influence can still be seen today.

1. The word fine in the passage is closest in meaning to

   (A) exact

   (B) bright

   (C) boring

   (D) excellent

2. Why does the author mention Monet?

   (A) To show the Impressionists' interest in the effects of light

   (B) To suggest that some Impressionists tended to avoid using bright colors

   (C) To explain how the Impressionists' techniques influenced other artists

   (D) To introduce a creative technique used by a popular Impressionist painter

3. In paragraphs 1 and 2, the author explains the characteristics of Impressionism by

   (A) illustrating how the style is used by artists today

   (B) describing the most famous Impressionist paintings

   (C) contrasting them with those of traditional French art

   (D) showing how they were influenced by other artistic styles

   Paragraphs 1 and 2 are marked with arrows [➡].

4. According to paragraph 3, why did Impressionism gain popularity?

   (A) It was praised by many art critics.

   (B) It offered artists new creative freedom.

   (C) It was supported by several famous artists.

   (D) It was easy to understand for the general public.

   Paragraph 3 is marked with an arrow [➡].

5. **Directions:** An introductory sentence for a brief summary of the passage is provided below. Complete the summary by selecting the THREE answer choices that express the most important ideas in the passage. Some sentences do not belong in the summary because they express ideas that are not presented in the passage or are minor ideas in the passage.

Impressionism was different in important ways from traditional French art.

-
-
-

Answer Choices

Ⓐ Renoir, Monet, Sisley, and Bazille were major Impressionist painters in France.

Ⓑ The Impressionist painters focused on the effects of light on their subjects.

Ⓒ The Impressionist painters tried to express their individual view of their subjects at a specific moment.

Ⓓ Paintings were always done indoors like studios.

Ⓔ Art critics gave poor reviews to the works of the Impressionists.

Ⓕ Impressionism spread throughout the art world, and it remains important today.

Vocabulary Review

A   Choose the correct word for each definition.

> Ⓐ term   Ⓑ artificial   Ⓒ input
>
> Ⓓ claw   Ⓔ critic   Ⓕ face

1. one who judges others' work: _____
2. to be positioned toward something: _____
3. made by copying a natural product: _____
4. a word or phrase that has an exact meaning: _____
5. a sharp nail at the end of an animal's toe: _____

B   Choose the best synonym for each pair of words.

> Ⓐ field   Ⓑ considerable   Ⓒ gap
>
> Ⓓ extend   Ⓔ pore   Ⓕ circumstance

1. large   great   : _____
2. space   opening   : _____
3. stretch   reach   : _____
4. situation   condition : _____

C   Fill in the blanks with the best answer.

> temperature   unpredictable   individual   details   lower

1. The company decided to _____ the price of its products.
2. I called Serena to get the _____ about the meeting I missed.
3. On Everest, _____ weather may delay climbers' schedules.
4. The _____ dropped to minus 20 degrees this winter.

D Choose the word that is closest in meaning to each highlighted word.

1. The medication can produce a feeling of depression and anxiety.
   - (A) promote
   - (B) build
   - (C) cause
   - (D) offer

2. Your leg bones should be strong enough to support the weight of your body.
   - (A) provide
   - (B) assist
   - (C) change
   - (D) bear

3. A number of Schubert's works were left incomplete, such as his Symphony No. 8.
   - (A) unfinished
   - (B) performed
   - (C) unlocked
   - (D) untouched

4. The director of the play tried to capture the mood of the audience.
   - (A) force
   - (B) catch
   - (C) raise
   - (D) gather

E Choose the opposite meaning of each highlighted word.

1. We have specific issues to discuss today.
   - (A) general
   - (B) unimportant
   - (C) few
   - (D) urgent

2. Her car problem was obviously related to the cold weather.
   - (A) closely
   - (B) mainly
   - (C) simply
   - (D) unclearly

3. In the park, Sonya released her dog to allow it to run free.
   - (A) watched
   - (B) guarded
   - (C) discouraged
   - (D) held

F Choose the correct phrase to complete each sentence.

1. Victims of the flood now (pass along / number in) the thousands.
2. Many animals lost their habitat (with respect to / as a result of) the forest fire.
3. The attitudes of my friends (have an influence on / give in) how I feel and act.

UNIT

Reference

■ Reference questions ask you to find the word or phrase that a pronoun refers to.

QUESTION TYPES

• The word ☐ in the passage refers to

• The phrase ☐ in the passage refers to

Constellations are patterns of stars in the night sky that form simple figures or shapes. People used these star patterns for a variety of purposes. One of the earliest uses was agricultural. Before they had calendars, farmers used the movement of 5 constellations to track the changing seasons. The stars helped them make decisions about when to plant their crops and when to harvest them. When the constellation Orion, for example, could be easily seen in the sky, farmers knew winter was approaching. Another way constellations assisted people was in navigation. For instance, the constellation Ursa Minor helped sailors quickly 10 locate the important navigational marker Polaris. Polaris is almost directly in line with the North Pole, so it does not appear to move in the sky during the course of the night or year. Thus, sailors relied on it to know where to go.

1   The word them in the passage refers to
(A) constellations
(B) calendars
(C) farmers
(D) seasons

2   The word it in the passage refers to
(A) Ursa Minor
(B) Polaris
(C) North Pole
(D) sky

Snow rollers are a natural phenomenon in which snow is rolled by wind in cylindrical shapes. They occur in many sizes. They can occasionally be seen in winter in North America and northern Europe. Snow rollers are rare because it takes an unusual 5 combination of snow and wind to make them. They can only be made with a special type of snow. It[1] must be wet and sticky but loose on top, with drier, lighter snow underneath. When there is thick snow on the ground, the sun sometimes melts the top layer enough to produce this special kind of snow. Additionally, the wind must be blowing strongly enough to move the snow, but not so 10 strongly that it[2] breaks up a roller. If the snow starts rolling downhill, even a gentle wind can get a snow roller started and gravity can continue rolling it to make it bigger. Snow rollers are an interesting phenomenon that scientists study to try to understand weather conditions.

1 The word It[1] in the passage refers to

(A) snow roller

(B) snow

(C) winter

(D) ground

2 The word it[2] in the passage refers to

(A) thick snow

(B) sun

(C) wind

(D) gravity

The Great Chicago Fire

→ Chicago had grown rapidly in the years between 1850 and 1870, expanding to around 300,000 residents. Many of its houses and other buildings were simple wooden structures which were built quickly to make room for people moving in. The summer and fall of 1871 were unusually dry, with only a couple of inches of rainfall. The conditions were right for a major fire to start, and it did so on the night of October 8, 5 1871.

→ No one knows for sure where or how the fire started. Flames were first seen near the barn of Catherine O'Leary, who lived on Chicago's West Side. Later reports said that one of her cows had kicked over an oil lamp and started the fire, but this is most likely a legend. High winds and the wooden structures of the city helped the fire 10 spread quickly to other neighborhoods. Soon, it had crossed the river and reached the center of the city. It burned for a day and a half until rain on the morning of October 10 succeeded in putting it out.

The damage caused by the fire was enormous. About three hundred people were killed, and a third of the city's population was left homeless. The fire destroyed 15 more than 70,000 buildings, including many important downtown government offices. However, the local authorities put great effort into rebuilding, and within a few years they had gotten the city back on its feet.

1 According to paragraph 1, many of Chicago's buildings were simple wooden structures because

Ⓐ the city's residents were not wealthy

Ⓑ this was the fashion of the period

Ⓒ they needed to be built in a short time

Ⓓ stronger structures were not necessary in the dry climate

Paragraph 1 is marked with an arrow [→].

2 The word It in the passage refers to

Ⓐ wooden structure

Ⓑ fire

Ⓒ river

Ⓓ city center

3 In paragraph 2, why does the author mention Catherine O'Leary's cow?

Ⓐ To explain why the fire spread so rapidly

Ⓑ To give an example of the damage that the fire caused

Ⓒ To introduce a story about the start of the Chicago fire

Ⓓ To suggest that there was little development on Chicago's West Side

Paragraph 2 is marked with an arrow [→].

4 The word its in the passage refers to

Ⓐ damage

Ⓑ fire

Ⓒ rebuilding effort

Ⓓ city

🖻 **SUMMARY**

Chicago experienced rapid growth between 1850 and 1870, with many simple _____

structures being quickly constructed. An almost rainless period created the perfect conditions

for the _____ that started on October 8, 1871. Its origins are unknown, but high

_____ allowed the fire to spread quickly through the wooden buildings. It burned for

a day and a half before rain put it out. It resulted in about 300 deaths, left a third of the city's

population _____, and destroyed more than 70,000 _____. A strong rebuilding

effort, however, restored the city within a few years.

Separation Anxiety

Babies go through many developmental stages as they grow, and there are certain behaviors related to each stage. One of these is the development of separation anxiety. If a child becomes upset when he or she is separated from a parent or other primary caregiver, the child is experiencing separation anxiety. 5

When babies are first born, they do not feel separation anxiety. In the first few months of life, they are unable to recognize the differences between caregivers. As long as their basic needs are met, they will be happy under anyone's care. Then, at around seven months of age, babies begin to understand that there are special 10 people who usually take care of them – most often, their parents – and they learn to recognize them. However, they are not able to understand the concept of time yet. Therefore, when their parents leave them, they feel that these important caregivers may never come back. They become very upset, even if they are left alone for only a few seconds. To prevent their parents from going away, they cry and cling. 15

From age 2, children come to understand that their parents will always return to them after an absence. With this knowledge, their feelings of separation anxiety usually disappear. Although some continue to experience anxiety over separation, it does not last for the entire time the parent is gone.

1 The word them in the passage refers to
- Ⓐ differences between caregivers
- Ⓑ basic needs
- Ⓒ babies
- Ⓓ special people

2 The word it in the passage refers to

(A) absence

(B) knowledge

(C) anxiety

(D) separation

3 **Directions:** An introductory sentence for a brief summary of the passage is provided below. Complete the summary by selecting the THREE answer choices that express the most important ideas in the passage.

Separation anxiety is a natural developmental stage that babies experience.

-
-
-

Answer Choices

(A) Children who feel separation anxiety think that their parents will return after a long time.

(B) Babies do not experience separation anxiety very early in life.

(C) Separation anxiety usually starts when babies can recognize their parents but do not understand the concept of time.

(D) Babies use certain behaviors to convince their parents not to leave them.

(E) Once babies realize that their parents will return, their anxiety goes away.

(F) Some children continue to suffer from separation anxiety after age two.

ORGANIZATION

- Separation anxiety
  - babies become _____ when they are separated from their caregivers
- Causes of separation anxiety
  - at around _____ months, children begin to _____ their primary caregivers
  - when primary caregivers leave, children fear that they will not come back
- The end of the separation anxiety stage
  - disappears when children realize primary caregivers will _____

The Disappearance of a Lake

In May of 2007, workers in the Bernardo O'Higgins National Park in Chile found that one of the park's lakes had disappeared. The 20,000-square-meter, 30-meter-deep lake in the southern Andes Mountains had been seen just two months earlier by a survey team. But in May, all that was left were some pieces of ice from the lake's surface.   5

Theories were quickly developed about how the lake had disappeared. One suggested that an earthquake was responsible. This region of Chile experiences earthquakes all the time, and a large one was reported on April 21. The earthquake could have produced cracks in the ground under the lake and caused the water to empty into them. Another theory discussed the lake's dams, which were made of ice.   10 These natural dams formed the lake by trapping its water. If the ice dams had melted or broken for some reason, they would have released the water lying behind them.

→ After a month or more of research, scientists learned that the lake's ice dams had indeed broken. All the water in the lake came from the melting of two nearby glaciers in the Andes Mountains. However, global warming caused these glaciers to   15 melt faster and faster. Finally, in May of 2007, they fed too much water into the lake. The ice dams could not hold it all and they broke, sending the lake's water down the mountains and into the sea.

1   Why does the author mention that a large one was reported on April 21?
   (A) To show one of the frequently occuring natural disasters in Chile
   (B) To describe how a crack was created in the ground at the lake's bottom
   (C) To discuss why scientists were unable to explain the lake's disappearance
   (D) To explain why some people blamed an earthquake for the disappearance of the lake

2   The word them in the passage refers to

    Ⓐ earthquakes

    Ⓑ cracks

    Ⓒ natural dams

    Ⓓ lakes

3   The word they in the passage refers to

    Ⓐ scientists

    Ⓑ ice dams

    Ⓒ glaciers

    Ⓓ Andes Mountains

4   According to paragraph 3, all of the following are facts that scientists learned about the lake's disappearance EXCEPT

    Ⓐ melting glaciers supplied the lake's water

    Ⓑ too much water caused the ice dams to break

    Ⓒ the mountain glaciers had been melting faster than usual

    Ⓓ the lake's ice dams were suddenly melted by global warming

Paragraph 3 is marked with an arrow [➜].

🗐 SUMMARY

In May of 2007, a(n) _____ in a national park in Chile disappeared. One theory was that a(n) _____ produced cracks in the ground beneath the lake, causing it to empty. Another theory suggested that natural _____ _____ had either broken or melted, allowing the lake to empty. This turned out to be correct. _____ _____ had increased the melting rate of two nearby _____, adding a lot of water to the lake. As a result, the ice dams eventually broke.

iBT PRACTICE

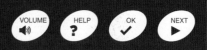

An Unusual Ocean Creature: the Jellyfish

→ The jellyfish gets its name from its jelly-like appearance. Despite their name, however, jellyfish are not fish. They are actually relatives of corals. They can be found in all the oceans of the world, and some even live in freshwater lakes and rivers.

→ Because they are 95 percent water and have no heart, blood, or brain, jellyfish are almost see-through. Their body shape looks like a bell with a *diameter of between 3 millimeters and 2 meters. On the underside of the bell, there is one or more mouths. Along with the bell, jellyfish also have tentacles that hang from under their body. The tentacles look like long, thin arms and are used to catch food. One of the largest jellyfish, the lion's mane jellyfish, has tentacles over 30 meters long.

Generally drifting with the waves, jellyfish have a limited ability to control movement. They use special muscles to pull water into their bell and push it out again. The motion is similar to an umbrella being slowly opened and closed. When this happens, the jellyfish shoots up like a rocket.

To get energy, jellyfish feed on small animals such as shrimp and plankton. Some of them even eat jellyfish of other species. However, they cannot carry too much in their bodies for long because it would increase their weight, making it difficult to keep floating. Therefore, jellyfish digest their food and get rid of waste very quickly.

Though mostly harmless to humans, certain jellyfish have been known to give deadly stings. These poisonous stings come from cells called *nematocysts,* which shoot out like small arrows into prey. When a dangerous jellyfish stings someone, that person can die in less than three minutes.

*diameter: the length of a straight line passing through the center of a circle from one side to the other

1. The word appearance in the passage is closest in meaning to

   (A) movement

   (B) function

   (C) characteristic

   (D) look

2. According to paragraphs 1 and 2, which of the following is true of jellyfish?

   (A) They are considered to be a kind of fish.

   (B) They are not found in rivers.

   (C) They have a simple heart and brain.

   (D) They use tentacles to hunt.

   Paragraphs 1 and 2 are marked with arrows [➞].

3. The word it in the passage refers to

   (A) bell

   (B) muscle

   (C) water

   (D) umbrella

4. The author mentions umbrella in order to

   (A) suggest how big jellyfish are

   (B) describe the movement of jellyfish

   (C) explain how jellyfish protect themselves

   (D) show how jellyfish carry food in their body

5. Which of the sentences below best expresses the essential information in the highlighted sentence in the passage? *Incorrect* choices change the meaning in important ways or leave out essential information.

   Ⓐ They can float well in the water when their weight is light.

   Ⓑ Because of their diet, jellyfish have many problems floating in the ocean.

   Ⓒ Too much food makes them too heavy to float well, so they cannot carry food for long.

   Ⓓ They cannot digest heavy food because they must use their energy to keep floating.

6. The word harmless in the passage is closest in meaning to

   Ⓐ safe

   Ⓑ useful

   Ⓒ familiar

   Ⓓ valuable

Vocabulary Review

A   Choose the correct word for each definition.

> (A) caregiver   (B) creature   (C) legend
>
> (D) navigation   (E) approach   (F) crack

1. to come closer: _____
2. one who looks after someone else: _____
3. a narrow space between two parts of a thing: _____
4. the act of planning a route for a ship and other vehicles: _____
5. an old story, often about a well-known person or event: _____

B   Choose the best synonym for each pair of words.

> (A) entire   (B) assist   (C) species
>
> (D) figure   (E) related   (F) track

1. complete   whole : _____
2. associated   linked : _____
3. shape   form   : _____
4. aid   help   : _____

C   Fill in the blanks with the best answer.

> phenomenon   melt   absence   harvest   digest

1. The farmer plans to _____ the apples in the fall.
2. Spring is coming and the snow is starting to _____.
3. Cows have special stomachs that help them _____ grass.
4. A volcanic eruption is a natural _____ that occurs all around the world.

D Choose the word that is closest in meaning to each highlighted word.

1. Anne lives in an enormous house with seven rooms.
   Ⓐ expensive   Ⓑ old   Ⓒ huge   Ⓓ modern

2. Bill had indeed done an excellent job on the project.
   Ⓐ finally   Ⓑ truly   Ⓒ lately   Ⓓ successfully

3. Many of the town's residents showed up to vote for the next president.
   Ⓐ officers   Ⓑ citizens   Ⓒ soldiers   Ⓓ employees

4. I heard that there are only a limited number of tickets available for the game.
   Ⓐ large   Ⓑ unknown   Ⓒ desired   Ⓓ restricted

E Choose the opposite meaning of each highlighted word.

1. The child thought the paper boat would float, but it didn't.
   Ⓐ appear   Ⓑ stop   Ⓒ sink   Ⓓ sail

2. The species of insect is so rare that only a few people have actually seen it.
   Ⓐ common   Ⓑ useless   Ⓒ regular   Ⓓ actual

3. Mom asked me to empty the waste basket in my room.
   Ⓐ fill up   Ⓑ remove   Ⓒ bring   Ⓓ take out

F Choose the correct phrase to complete each sentence.

1. Teenagers (go through / set out) physical and psychological changes.
2. Firefighters and volunteers tried for days to (burn up / put out) the huge forest fire.
3. Teeth help to (break up / leave out) food into smaller pieces and the tongue helps to swallow it.

Fact & Negative Fact

■ **Factual Information**
Factual Information questions ask about important details in the passage.

■ **Negative Fact**
Negative Fact questions ask you to identify information that is incorrect or is not mentioned in the passage.

QUESTION TYPES

Factual Information
• According to the passage, which of the following is true about X?
• According to paragraph _, when / why / how ...?
• According to paragraph _, X occurred because

Negative Fact
• According to the passage, which of the following is NOT true of X?
• Which of the following is NOT mentioned as X?
• All of the following are mentioned as X EXCEPT

When a person shouts, sound waves travel through the air. The process is similar to the way *ripples of water move through a lake. When the waves reach your ears, you hear a sound. But if those sound waves come into contact with an object or surface, 5 such as the walls of a cave, they are reflected into the air. When this sound bounces back toward your ears, you hear it again as an echo. This second sound can only be heard when there is a certain distance between the object or surface in question and your ears. If the gap is too small, the echo occurs too quickly to be heard. In order for an echo to be clear, the sound must reflect off an 10 object or surface at least 16.2 meters away. This is why you cannot hear an echo if you shout in a small room, even though the noise reflects off the walls.

*ripple: a small wave on the surface of water

1   According to the passage, sound waves bounce back into the air when they
     Ⓐ reach a person's ear
     Ⓑ meet an object or surface
     Ⓒ come in contact with a lake
     Ⓓ run into louder sound waves

2   According to the passage, why can't you hear an echo in a small room?
     Ⓐ Because the echo returns to your ears too quickly
     Ⓑ Because sound waves become weaker in small spaces
     Ⓒ Because noise reflects off walls faster than other surfaces
     Ⓓ Because sound waves do not reflect into the air in small rooms

BASIC DRILLS 02

Located between Jordan and Israel, the Dead Sea is not a sea at all, but rather a salt lake. At about 400 meters below sea level, the Dead Sea is the lowest-lying body of water on Earth. Water from the Jordan River flows into it from the north, while other smaller ⁵ streams run into it from the east. However, as the Dead Sea lies lower than the surrounding land, it has no exit. This means that water only escapes the lake through the process of evaporation. High temperatures evaporate the water just as quickly as it flows into the lake. As water disappears, salt, along with other minerals contained in the water, are left behind. Over time, these minerals have ¹⁰ built up, resulting in a lake with nearly nine times the ocean's salt content. Any fish coming from the Jordan River die as soon as they enter the Dead Sea. Therefore, there is almost no life in the lake except for a few small organisms.

1   According to the passage, which of the following is true of the Dead Sea?
   (A) It is the deepest lake in the world.
   (B) It lies lower than any other body of water on Earth.
   (C) The Jordan River is its only source of water.
   (D) It loses water through several small streams.

2   According to the passage, almost no life can survive in the Dead Sea because
   (A) it contains too much salt
   (B) it has too high of a temperature
   (C) it receives polluted water from the Jordan River
   (D) it has no source of food for fish

The Washington Monument

→ The Washington Monument is located in Washington, D.C., the capital of the United States of America. It was constructed in the nineteenth century to honor George Washington, the first president of the United States. The monument is one of the tallest monuments in the world, standing at 555 feet. The tall, narrow structure is white and obelisk-shaped with four sides that join in a pyramid-like top. 5

→ The idea for the Washington Monument came from Pierre Charles L'Enfant, an architect who was involved in designing the city of Washington, D.C. Although many people supported his idea, deciding what to build was difficult. This led to the foundation of the Washington National Monument Society. In 1836, the organization held a design competition which was won by architect Robert Mills. Judges favored 10 Mills's design because it showed both simplicity and grandness, two qualities George Washington was known for. The construction started in 1848, but it was paused because of a lack of funds. The Civil War further delayed the project. It was not until 1876, when the U.S. Congress agreed to fund the completion of the monument, that construction was finally restarted. Finally, in 1884, the Washington Monument was 15 completed and opened to the public. Today, the monument is one of the most famous tourist attractions in the United States and attracts visitors from all over the world.

1 According to paragraph 1, which of the following is NOT true about the Washington Monument?

(A) It is shaped exactly like a pyramid.

(B) It is located in the capital of the United States.

(C) It is one of the tallest monuments in the world.

(D) It was created in honor of the first U.S. president.

Paragraph 1 is marked with an arrow [→].

2 The word foundation in the passage is closest in meaning to

Ⓐ change Ⓑ donation Ⓒ formation Ⓓ suggestion

3 Why does the author mention the U.S. Congress?

Ⓐ To show how the project finally received funds

Ⓑ To explain why the citizens wanted to finish the construction

Ⓒ To describe the difficulty of funding the monument's construction

Ⓓ To suggest that the Civil War changed people's opinion of the construction of the monument

4 According to paragraph 2, why was Robert Mills's design chosen?

Ⓐ Because it had an unusual and memorable shape

Ⓑ Because it represented some of George Washington's qualities

Ⓒ Because it was more economical to build than the other designs

Ⓓ Because it matched the environment of Washington, D.C. well

Paragraph 2 is marked with an arrow [➡].

SUMMARY

The Washington Monument in Washington, D.C. was constructed in honor of President _____ _____ in the nineteenth century. At 555 feet, it is one of the _____ monuments in the world. It was the idea of the architect Pierre Charles L'Enfant, who helped design the city of Washington, D.C. A design _____ was held, which was won by Robert Mills for his simple, yet grand design. A lack of funds, followed by the _____ _____, delayed construction. However, the monument was finally completed in _____.

Ants and Termites

Many people think that ants and termites are the same insect with different body colors. Because of this, termites are popularly but incorrectly known as "white ants." However, the two insects are actually different species. Termites are closely related to cockroaches and can be distinguished from ants in several ways.

→ The clearest physical difference between ants and termites is that while ants   5 have three body parts – a head, *thorax and *abdomen, termites have only a head and thorax. Furthermore, while ants have curved antennae, termites have short, straight antennae. Ants have two compound eyes, which are made up of many smaller eyes, to help them find food above ground. However, most termites do not have eyes. Instead, they rely on their other senses like smell and touch to guide them. Finally, both species   10 have six legs, but ants have longer legs than termites.

→ In addition to physical features, there are many other characteristics that separate ants from termites. Ants eat almost anything but most termites feed only on wood. Their habitats also can be quite different, as ants live in a variety of places but termites do not. Some ants do not build permanent nests at all, and others   15 create mounds made up of dirt and plant materials. Termites, on the other hand, cannot endure living out in the open because their bodies are more sensitive to the environment. Therefore, they must construct stronger and more complex habitats where they can control the temperature and humidity of their environment.

*thorax: the middle section of an insect's body
*abdomen: the lower section of an insect's body

1 Why does the author mention white ants?
   Ⓐ To explain the physical appearance of termites
   Ⓑ To give an example of another name for termites
   Ⓒ To emphasize the similarities between ants and termites
   Ⓓ To point out a common misunderstanding about termites

2   The phrase rely on in the passage is closest in meaning to

  Ⓐ display   Ⓑ prefer

  Ⓒ depend on   Ⓓ bring up

3   According to paragraph 2, which of the following is NOT a physical difference
     between ants and termites?

  Ⓐ Termites have two body sections, but ants have three.

  Ⓑ Ants have curved antennae, but termites have straight ones.

  Ⓒ Ants have compound eyes, while most termites have no eyes.

  Ⓓ Termites have longer legs than ants.

  Paragraph 2 is marked with an arrow [➡].

4   According to paragraph 3, why do termites build stronger and more complex
     habitats than ants?

  Ⓐ Because they have more enemies than ants

  Ⓑ Because they live in larger communities than ants

  Ⓒ Because they have better building techniques than ants

  Ⓓ Because they are unable to live unprotected in the open

  Paragraph 3 is marked with an arrow [➡].

🗐 ORGANIZATION

- Physical differences between ants and termites
    - ants have _____ body parts; termites have two
    - antennae of ants are _____; antennae of termites are straight
    - ants have _____ eyes; most termites are eyeless
    - the legs of ants are _____ than those of termites
- Behavioral differences between ants and termites
    - most termites eat only _____; ants eat a wide variety of food
    - termites must live in controlled environments; ants live in a wide variety of habitats

READING **PRACTICE 03**

The Mystery of the Indus Valley Civilization

 ➡ The Indus Valley Civilization was one of the world's earliest civilizations, like those in Egypt, Mesopotamia, and China. It appears to have begun around 2600 BC. The civilization included a vast number of settlements built on the banks of the Indus ⁵ River and surrounding areas. It is also known as the Harappan Civilization, named after the ancient city called Harappa that archaeologists discovered in the 1920s.

The people of the Indus Valley were very advanced. Houses were made from fired bricks and stood between one and three stories high. Each house had its own private ¹⁰ bathroom, which was connected by clay pipes to an efficient sewer system that took wastewater out of the house. The cities' roads were arranged in a *grid, showing that they were carefully planned by skillful engineers.

This advanced civilization existed for about 900 years, but around 1700 BC, it disappeared. People left the cities suddenly, and no one knows for sure why this ¹⁵ happened. Perhaps there was a natural disaster like a flood or an earthquake, or maybe they were defeated by another civilization. The most likely theory is that climate change caused the collapse of the civilization. Researchers have worked hard to find clues, but the truth about the Indus Valley Civilization is still a mystery.

grid: a system of straight lines that cross each other to form squares

1 According to paragraph 1, the Harappan Civilization gets its name from

    Ⓐ one of its cities

    Ⓑ a nearby river

    Ⓒ the archaeologist who discovered it

    Ⓓ the country in which it was located

Paragraph 1 is marked with an arrow [➡].

2 Which of the sentences below best expresses the essential information in the highlighted sentence in the passage?

- (A) The private bathrooms of houses were connected to a sewer system.
- (B) In addition to having their own bathrooms, houses were connected by clay pipes.
- (C) The sewer system was used to get rid of the waste from each house.
- (D) Although the houses were equipped with private bathrooms, they had no method for removing wastewater.

3 The word they in the passage refers to

- (A) houses
- (B) clay pipes
- (C) roads
- (D) engineers

4 According to the passage, all of the following are true of the Indus Valley Civilization EXCEPT

- (A) it is one of the oldest civilizations in history
- (B) it may have been destroyed by climate change
- (C) its cities included many features that are considered advanced for the time
- (D) its historic site was all discovered in 1700 BC

🖸 ORGANIZATION

- The Indus Valley Civilization
  - began around 2600 BC and is also known as the _____ Civilization
- Advanced urban development
  - houses were made from fired _____ and stood up to three stories high
  - used an indoor sewer system
  - _____ were arranged in a grid
- The end of the Indus Valley Civilization
  - disappeared around 1700 BC
  - reason for its collapse is a(n) _____

The Paintings of Lascaux

The Lascaux cave is located in the Bordeaux region of southwestern France. This cave is famous for its 17,000-year old cave paintings. They show that art has been a part of human life since prehistoric times, and are considered to be one of the greatest works of ancient art ever found.

→ The cave walls are decorated with red, yellow, brown, and black paintings. 5 There are about 2,000 figures in all, and the most common themes are wild animals. More than 600 of the figures have been identified as specific animals, such as horses, deer, birds, and bulls. In the paintings, these animals are seen in a variety of poses, including with heads turned, walking in water, and falling off cliffs. They are surprisingly realistic. The sizes of the animals are quite large. For example, one 10 of the bulls in the paintings is 17 feet long. In contrast to the figures of animals, very few pictures of humans are found in Lascaux. These human images are small compared to the animal images and roughly drawn.

→ It is not clear why ancient artists painted images of animals in the cave of Lascaux. However, most people agree that the Lascaux cave paintings were more 15 than decoration. This is because the cave itself does not have any signs of being lived in. Moreover, the paintings are often drawn in parts of the cave that are difficult to get to. Therefore, they are thought to have served very special purposes. Since human figures in the paintings have weapons, some scholars suggest that they functioned as an instructional guide to hunting. Another theory suggests that the 20 cave paintings were part of religious or social events. It may have been that the act of painting itself was more important than the finished paintings.

1. The word functioned in the passage is closest in meaning to

    (A) failed   (B) worked

    (C) settled   (D) developed

2. According to paragraphs 2 and 3, which of the following is true about the human images?

    (A) They are shown carrying weapons.

    (B) They are seen in various poses.

    (C) They were the main theme of the paintings.

    (D) They are larger than the animal images.

    Paragraphs 2 and 3 are marked with arrows [→].

3. According to paragraph 3, which of the following is a reason why the Lascaux paintings were not just decoration?

    (A) Because the paintings of animals were unrealistic

    (B) Because the paintings were used for hunting ceremonies

    (C) Because there is no evidence that people lived in the cave

    (D) Because the paintings are only located at the entrance of the cave

    Paragraph 3 is marked with an arrow [→].

4. What can be inferred from the passage about ancient people?

    (A) They spent most of their time painting figures.

    (B) They did not know how to successfully hunt animals.

    (C) Animals were closely related to their lives.

    (D) Caves were their most important places of residence.

5. **Directions:** An introductory sentence for a brief summary of the passage is provided below. Complete the summary by selecting the THREE answer choices that express the most important ideas in the passage. Some sentences do not belong in the summary because they express ideas that are not presented in the passage or are minor ideas in the passage.

> The Lascaux cave in France contains many early human art works.
>
> •
>
> •
>
> •

Answer Choices

Ⓐ The act of painting was an aspect of prehistoric social events.

Ⓑ The walls of the Lascaux caves show scenes of wild animals and humans.

Ⓒ The paintings were created to provide an instructional guide to hunting.

Ⓓ There are about 2,000 images of wild animals, including horses, deer, and bulls.

Ⓔ The paintings are thought to have served some special purposes.

Ⓕ The paintings are ranked as one of the most important examples of prehistoric art.

Vocabulary Review

A Choose the correct word for each definition.

Ⓐ habitat	Ⓑ efficient	Ⓒ instructional
Ⓓ humidity	Ⓔ physical	Ⓕ monument

1. related to the body: _____
2. a living space of an animal or plant: _____
3. a structure built in honor of a person: _____
4. the amount of water in the air: _____
5. working without wasting time, money, or energy: _____

B Choose the best synonym for each pair of words or phrases.

Ⓐ delay	Ⓑ reflect	Ⓒ identify
Ⓓ vast	Ⓔ connect	Ⓕ polluted

1. put off   postpone : _____
2. link   join   : _____
3. huge   enormous : _____
4. dirty   unclean   : _____

C Fill in the blanks with the best answer.

figure	advanced	architect	judges	roughly

1. The artist _____ sketched the outlines of the scene.
2. The player revealed a new _____ technique during the game.
3. The building was designed by the great _____ Frank Lloyd Wright.
4. All of the _____ at the competition agreed that Ann's performance was perfect.

D   Choose the word that is closest in meaning to each highlighted word.

1. We arranged the books in the library by subject and title yesterday.

   Ⓐ organized   Ⓑ labelled   Ⓒ studied   Ⓓ collected

2. There was a mound of dirt beside the hole in the ground.

   Ⓐ ball   Ⓑ hill   Ⓒ collection   Ⓓ piece

3. Eventually, the soldiers were able to defeat their enemies.

   Ⓐ monitor   Ⓑ block   Ⓒ meet   Ⓓ beat

4. The beautiful national park attracts thousands of visitors every summer.

   Ⓐ holds   Ⓑ allows   Ⓒ expects   Ⓓ draws

E   Choose the opposite meaning of each highlighted word.

1. Thomas took a picture of the curved street in his neighborhood.

   Ⓐ dirty   Ⓑ straight   Ⓒ narrow   Ⓓ crowded

2. It is interesting that Canadian geese have a permanent mate for life.

   Ⓐ single   Ⓑ chosen   Ⓒ temporary   Ⓓ new

3. Our town's city hall was constructed in the eighteenth century.

   Ⓐ destroyed   Ⓑ rebuilt   Ⓒ decorated   Ⓓ closed

F   Choose the correct phrase to complete each sentence.

1. (In contrast to / In favor of) her brother, Jenny is very tall.
2. Human blood is (made out / made up of) several different types of cells.
3. A newly found star was (completed by / named after) a Spanish astronomer.

UNIT
04

Sentence Simplification

- Sentence Simplification questions ask you to choose the best summary of a sentence from the passage.

BASIC DRILLS 01

Blood pressure is the force of blood pushing against the walls of the arteries, the tubes that carry blood from the heart to the rest of the body. With each beat of the heart, blood is pumped into the arteries and the force of blood pressure is at its highest. This 5 is called systolic pressure. On the other hand, when the heart is resting, between beats, your blood pressure is much lower – this is called diastolic pressure. As you can see, what we normally call "blood pressure" is really the combination of these two types of pressure: systolic and diastolic. Though blood pressure is different from day to day, as long as the systolic pressure is less than 120 10 and the diastolic pressure is less than 80, the blood pressure is normal.

1 Which of the sentences below best expresses the essential information in the first highlighted sentence in the passage?
Ⓐ In the body, blood moves through tubes that are referred to as arteries.
Ⓑ The force of blood against the walls of blood-carrying tubes is blood pressure.
Ⓒ When blood travels through arteries, blood pressure is formed.
Ⓓ Blood pressure is the force that moves blood through the body.

2 Which of the sentences below best expresses the essential information in the second highlighted sentence in the passage?
Ⓐ People should not have systolic pressure above 120 or diastolic pressure above 80.
Ⓑ The average person's blood pressure is between 80 and 120, and it varies daily.
Ⓒ Blood pressure may change from day to day, but it should not change much.
Ⓓ Blood pressure is standard when systolic pressure is under 120 and diastolic pressure is under 80.

BASIC DRILLS 02

Johannes Vermeer was a famous painter of the 17th century and one of the most important figures in Dutch painting. Many common characteristics are found among his works. A lot of them show his subjects standing or sitting by an open window, which provides the only source of light. Female subjects in Vermeer's paintings are typically going about their everyday tasks, such as playing an instrument, writing a letter, or doing housework. In addition, Vermeer drew his subjects in the foreground surprisingly large, the way they would appear in a close-up photograph. Interestingly, many of his works contained maps of the Netherlands or globes in the background. These are thought to either represent the Dutch provinces' struggle for independence or show respect for the Dutch style of painting.

1 Which of the sentences below best expresses the essential information in the first highlighted sentence in the passage?

Ⓐ Most of Vermeer's subjects were standing near a window.

Ⓑ Vermeer liked to draw open windows, which provide light in his paintings.

Ⓒ Vermeer's paintings often included light from a window, by which his subjects were located.

Ⓓ Light was important to Vermeer, who often worked by an open window.

2 Which of the sentences below best expresses the essential information in the second highlighted sentence in the passage?

Ⓐ Vermeer's paintings show that he was influenced by photographic techniques.

Ⓑ Vermeer liked to draw large subjects so that he could make his paintings look more interesting.

Ⓒ Close-up photography causes subjects in the foreground to appear very large.

Ⓓ Vermeer's paintings show subjects as they would look in a close-up photograph.

Paleoclimatology

The study of Earth's climate history is known as paleoclimatology. Scientists gather information about Earth's past climates by studying natural records known as proxies, which include materials such as ice sheets and ocean *sediments.

➡ Polar ice sheets are one important kind of proxy. They are made up of layers of snow that have built up over long periods of time, so they contain details about   5 conditions that existed in Earth's past. By analyzing the dust and air bubbles trapped inside the ice sheets, experts can create a picture of what the planet's climate used to be like. For example, they can assume how much snow fell, what kind of gases were in the atmosphere, or when volcanic activity occurred.

➡ In the same way, ocean sediments provide researchers with a key to climates   10 of the past. Like layers of ice, ocean sediments consist of layers that have built up over time. Sediments found in the ocean contain well-preserved fossils of sea creatures. Using the information found in fossils, scientists can determine the environmental conditions of ocean water where fossilized species lived, such as temperature and saltiness.   15

*sediment: sand, minerals, and soil that have been carried by water

1   Which of the sentences below best expresses the essential information in the highlighted sentence in paragraph 1?

Ⓐ Scientists use proxies to help them understand the Earth's past climates.

Ⓑ Some important kinds of proxies include ice sheets and ocean sediments.

Ⓒ The history of Earth's climates is difficult to study, so scientists use proxies.

Ⓓ Scientists study proxies to figure out the differences between Earth's past and present climates.

2   Which of the sentences below best expresses the essential information in the highlighted sentence in paragraph 2?

   Ⓐ Dust and air bubbles in ice sheets are the most useful evidence to determine Earth's past climates.

   Ⓑ It is possible to study the Earth's history with the help of ice sheets.

   Ⓒ When dust and air bubbles become trapped in ice, they preserve important information.

   Ⓓ Experts use dust and air bubbles in ice sheets to determine Earth's past climates.

3   The word assume in the passage is closest in meaning to

   Ⓐ show   Ⓑ prove

   Ⓒ guess   Ⓓ discuss

4   According to paragraphs 2 and 3, how are ice sheets and ocean sediments similar?

   Ⓐ They can both form in cold environments.

   Ⓑ They are both composed of layers that formed over time.

   Ⓒ They are both capable of preserving ancient animal fossils.

   Ⓓ They both provide information about the composition of the ocean.

Paragraphs 2 and 3 are marked with arrows [➡].

ORGANIZATION

- Paleoclimatology
  - the study of the history of the Earth's _____
  - data is gathered from studying natural records known as _____
- Polar ice sheets
  - made up of layers of _____
  - dust and air bubbles trapped in these layers give clues to past climate conditions
- Ocean sediments
  - _____ found in these sediments provide information on past ocean conditions

Jacques Cousteau

Born in 1910, Jacques Cousteau was a famous French explorer and researcher. He made great advancements in our knowledge of the Earth's oceans until his death in 1997. One of Cousteau's most important contributions to ocean science was the aqualung, which helped humans breathe ⁵ underwater. Cousteau and engineer Émile Gagnan developed the equipment in 1943. It allowed divers to go deeper and spend more time below the surface by controlling their air pressure at varying water depths.

In 1950, Cousteau began to travel all over the world in a research ship called the *Calypso*, visiting the waters of the Antarctic, Pacific, Atlantic, and Indian Ocean, as ¹⁰ well as the Nile, Amazon, and Mississippi River. Filming his journeys, he produced about 120 documentaries in all. They captured images of coral, sharks, penguins, and other forms of life that populate these underwater environments. These programs attracted audiences from all over the world. His documentaries made the public aware that human development was negatively affecting marine ecosystems and encouraged ¹⁵ people to be environmentally responsible.

1 Which of the sentences below best expresses the essential information in the highlighted sentence in paragraph 1?

Ⓐ Divers of Cousteau's time could not control air pressure underwater.

Ⓑ Before Cousteau's invention, divers had a hard time making deep, long dives.

Ⓒ It allowed divers to breathe underwater regardless of the air pressure.

Ⓓ It enabled divers to make deeper and longer dives by regulating their air pressure.

2 The word populate in the passage is closest in meaning to

(A) explore

(B) survive

(C) live in

(D) benefit from

3 Which of the sentences below best expresses the essential information in the highlighted sentence in paragraph 2?

(A) Cousteau's documentaries raised awareness and taught environmental responsibility.

(B) Cousteau's documentaries have been shown to influence the public's attitude toward environmental issues.

(C) Cousteau realized that it was important to make efforts to protect marine ecosystems.

(D) When Cousteau created his documentaries, marine ecosystems were in danger due to human development.

4 According to the passage, which of the following is NOT true about Jacques Cousteau?

(A) He invented an important underwater breathing device.

(B) He holds the record for the deepest ocean dive.

(C) He gave the public the opportunity to see underwater worlds.

(D) He produced educational documentaries while traveling the world.

SUMMARY

Jacques Cousteau was a French explorer who contributed greatly to our knowledge of the _____. He invented the aqualung in 1943, which controlled _____ _____ and allowed divers to make deeper and longer dives than ever before. In 1950, he began to travel around the world on his ship, the *Calypso*, and produced about 120 _____ about undersea life. His images raised public awareness of the harmful effects that humans have on marine _____.

The Four Forces of Flight

➜ There are four physical forces that are involved in the flight of airplanes. The first is thrust, which makes the airplane go forward. The plane's engines create thrust by pushing air backwards at great speed. Next, there is the force of drag, which pushes the plane backwards. ₅ It is usually the result of air resistance as the airplane moves forward through the air. The third force is lift, which is caused by the shape of the plane's wings. The top of each wing is curved and the bottom is flat. As the wings move forward, they force the air traveling over them to go faster than the air traveling under them, and this creates a force that lifts the wings up. Finally, there is weight, the opposite of lift. This is the force ₁₀ of gravity pulling the plane down towards the earth.

The airplane flies in a straight line and at a constant speed when these four forces are balanced. If they are unbalanced, the plane travels in the direction of the strongest force. For example, when thrust and lift are greater than drag and weight, the plane will accelerate and climb. On the other hand, if the plane loses thrust and lift, drag and ₁₅ weight will be stronger, forcing the plane to slow down and head towards the ground.

1 **Which of the sentences below best expresses the essential information in the highlighted sentence in paragraph 1?**

Ⓐ The difference in air speed above and below the wings produces lift.

Ⓑ Because of the wing design, an airplane can rise and move forward through the air.

Ⓒ Air travels at different speeds on either side of the wings.

Ⓓ When the force of the air above the plane is stronger than that below it, the plane's wings can move faster.

2   According to paragraph 1, all of the following are true about the four forces of flight EXCEPT

Ⓐ thrust is the opposite of drag

Ⓑ drag makes the airplane move forward

Ⓒ lift works against weight

Ⓓ weight is caused by the force of gravity

Paragraph 1 is marked with an arrow [➡].

3   The word accelerate in the passage is closest in meaning to

Ⓐ fall down   Ⓑ speed up

Ⓒ turn around   Ⓓ move ahead

4   Which of the sentences below best expresses the essential information in the highlighted sentence in paragraph 2?

Ⓐ It is the forces of thrust and lift that keep airplanes up in the air.

Ⓑ A heavier plane requires more thrust and lift in order to fly.

Ⓒ As the plane approaches the ground, drag and weight become stronger than thrust and lift.

Ⓓ When a plane does not create enough thrust and lift, it is pulled to the ground by drag and weight.

🗐 ORGANIZATION

- Tho four physical forces of flight

  - thrust is created by _____ and causes the airplane to move forward
  - drag is the air resistance that pushes the airplane _____
  - lift comes from the shape of the wings and moves the airplane upwards
  - weight is caused by _____ and pulls the airplane downward

- Balancing the four forces

  - when the forces are balanced, the airplane moves in a _____ line at a steady speed
  - when unbalanced, the airplane follows the direction of the _____ force

Copyleft

A creator can choose to have their work protected by a copyright. This means that the owner of the copyright is the only person or group that can produce copies of that work. But some creators want to make their work easier for people to use, change, and share. They apply a copyleft license to their work instead. A copyleft license allows people to use a piece of work freely. People may modify or distribute 5 material with a copyleft license, but whatever product they make must also have a copyleft license. This practice began in the software community in the early 1980s, but it has since been adopted by members of other industries, such as audio, visual, video, and educational content makers.

→ One area where copyleft licenses have been particularly successful is in 10 software development. A program's source code can be copylefted and easily shared with anyone who wishes to download a copy of it. People can then alter this source code to make a new program. This new program can legally be shared, but this modified source code must also be copylefted and made freely available to other users. Many programmers believe that copyleft licenses ensure that everyone 15 will have access to high-quality software. This is because a copyleft license prevents large corporations from buying a program's source code and controlling how it is used.

There are currently numerous copyleft projects either in use or in development, but not everyone supports this practice. Critics believe that copylefted material 20 could spread uncontrollably. Because all of the works that make use of copylefted material must also be copylefted, opponents say that it could cause the destruction of the concept of intellectual property.

TOEFL Reading

1. The word distribute in the passage is closest in meaning to

    Ⓐ possess

    Ⓑ remove

    Ⓒ manufacture

    Ⓓ circulate

2. Which of the sentences below best expresses the essential information in the following sentence? *Incorrect* choices change the meaning in important ways or leave out essential information.

    Ⓐ It is legal to share a program that has a copyleft license, but source code cannot be changed from its original form.

    Ⓑ Users may modify or share source code with a copyleft license, but the altered source code cannot then also be copylefted.

    Ⓒ Any program made by modifying copylefted source code may be legally shared, but the new program's source code must also have a copyleft license.

    Ⓓ Copylefted source code may be modified freely, but they cannot be shared with other users.

3. According to paragraph 2, why do some programmers support copyleft licenses?

    Ⓐ They think that it will allow them to develop software faster.

    Ⓑ They can gain access to source code owned by large corporations.

    Ⓒ They believe that it will lead to more people having better software.

    Ⓓ They want to own and control their source code exclusively.

    Paragraph 2 is marked with an arrow [➡].

4. Why does the author mention the destruction of the concept of intellectual property?

    Ⓐ To explain why some people oppose copyleft licenses

    Ⓑ To illustrate a major goal of the copyleft movement

    Ⓒ To suggest a solution to conflicts of intellectual ownership

    Ⓓ To highlight an area where copyleft licenses excel

5. **Directions:** An introductory sentence for a brief summary of the passage is provided below. Complete the summary by selecting the THREE answer choices that express the most important ideas in the passage. Some sentences do not belong in the summary because they express ideas that are not presented in the passage or are minor ideas in the passage.

> In contrast to a copyright, a copyleft license ensures that a piece of work is free to use.
>
> ●
>
> ●
>
> ●

Answer Choices

Ⓐ A copyright is used when content creators want to protect their work from other people.

Ⓑ The copylefted work is able to be modified and shared freely, but the modified work must also be.

Ⓒ Copyleft licenses are popular among software developers because they believe the licenses allow more people to use high-quality software.

Ⓓ Large corporations take advantage of copyleft licenses by purchasing the rights of softwares and then selling the programs.

Ⓔ While copyleft licenses have given people access to a large amount of source code, the numbers of copyleft projects remains very small.

Ⓕ Some people oppose copyleft licensing because they think that it will eventually prevent anyone from being able to own their own creations.

Vocabulary Review

A Choose the correct word for each definition.

> (A) accelerate   (B) analyze   (C) explorer
>
> (D) alter   (E) ensure   (F) expert

1. to study in detail: _____
2. to make sure that something happens: _____
3. to move faster or speed up: _____
4. one who travels to unfamiliar places: _____
5. one who knows a lot about a certain subject: _____

B Choose the best synonym for each pair of words.

> (A) respect   (B) assume   (C) layer
>
> (D) advancement   (E) varying   (F) task

1. guess   estimate   : _____
2. changing   different   : _____
3. duty   job   : _____
4. progress   improvement : _____

C Fill in the blanks with the best answer.

> breathe   encouraged   saltiness   independence   aware

1. The _____ of the water makes the body easier to float.
2. Mexico declared its _____ from Spain on September 16, 1810.
3. I was nervous about my speech, so I tried to _____ slowly and calmly.
4. The government _____ people to use public transportation to reduce air pollution.

D Choose the word that is closest in meaning to each highlighted word.

1. The combination of those two chemicals is dangerous.
   - (A) source
   - (B) use
   - (C) mix
   - (D) heat

2. Billy didn't want to miss the opportunity of becoming a singer.
   - (A) chance
   - (B) purpose
   - (C) effort
   - (D) future

3. They both want to modify the terms of their contract.
   - (A) discuss
   - (B) revise
   - (C) consider
   - (D) establish

4. She kept her plants healthy by regulating how much sunlight they received.
   - (A) deciding
   - (B) controlling
   - (C) knowing
   - (D) blocking

E Choose the opposite meaning of each highlighted word.

1. Most of the people in the city opposed the new economic plan.
   - (A) avoided
   - (B) resolved
   - (C) supported
   - (D) improved

2. I trapped the bug in a jar and brought it outside.
   - (A) found
   - (B) scared
   - (C) ignored
   - (D) released

3. The company decided to adopt a system with flexible working hours.
   - (A) reject
   - (B) reflect
   - (C) decline
   - (D) hide

F Choose the correct phrase to complete each sentence.

1. Water is being (pumped into / turned off) the swimming pool.
2. Our neighbors are (involved in / pulling out) an organization that helps the homeless.
3. I was (making fun of / going about) my morning routine when I heard a knock at the door.

Actual Practice Test

ACTUAL PRACTICE TEST 1

Three Layers of Skin

The skin consists of three layers. The outer layer is known as the epidermis. Its thickness is different depending on where on the body it is located. In areas such as the palms of the hands and undersides of the feet, it is 1.5 mm thick. In contrast, the thin skin of the eyelids is only 0.05 mm thick. Melanin-producing cells are located in the epidermis and give skin its color. The greater the amount of melanin contained in the epidermis, the darker a person's skin will be. In addition, Langerhans' cells are part of the epidermis. These cells help protect the body by detecting foreign substances that invade damaged skin.

→ Directly beneath the epidermis is the dermis. This is the thickest (1.5 – 4 mm) of the three skin layers. It accounts for about 90 percent of the skin's thickness. ■ A lot of nerve endings are contained within the dermis. ■ When your skin comes into contact with something, these nerve endings inform the brain about the object that they have touched. ■ Furthermore, small blood vessels in the dermis keep skin cells healthy by providing them with necessary oxygen and nutrients and removing waste. ■ The dermis also contains sweat glands that, in response to warm temperatures or exercise, produce sweat in order to cool the body. Oil glands in this layer release oil and moisten the skin. In addition, hair follicles, small holes where hair appears, can be found in this layer.

→ The deepest layer of the skin is known as the subcutaneous layer, or sometimes the hypodermis. Fat makes up the majority of this layer, which helps the body conserve heat and absorb shocks. The thickness of the subcutaneous layer varies across the body. It also differs from person to person. The blood vessels, nerves, and hair follicles also cross through this layer.

1. Why does the author mention melanin?

   Ⓐ To describe the structure of the epidermis

   Ⓑ To compare the characteristics of cells in the epidermis

   Ⓒ To stress the importance of melanin-producing cells

   Ⓓ To explain why people have different skin colors

2. The word foreign in the passage is closest in meaning to

   Ⓐ various   Ⓑ outside

   Ⓒ particular   Ⓓ dangerous

3. The phrase accounts for in the passage is closest in meaning to

   Ⓐ affects   Ⓑ makes up

   Ⓒ determines   Ⓓ presses down

4. The word them in the passage refers to

   Ⓐ nerve endings   Ⓑ small blood vessels

   Ⓒ skin cells   Ⓓ nutrients

5. Which of the sentences below best expresses the essential information in the highlighted sentence in the passage? *Incorrect* choices change the meaning in important ways or leave out essential information.

   Ⓐ Sweat glands in the dermis help cool the body by producing sweat.

   Ⓑ The dermis helps the body lower its temperature when necessary.

   Ⓒ Sweat is sometimes produced as a result of exercise or temperature.

   Ⓓ Special processes happen in the dermis in order to cool the body down.

6. According to paragraph 2, what is the role of blood vessels in the dermis?

    Ⓐ Maintaining a healthy body temperature

    Ⓑ Preventing diseases from invading the body

    Ⓒ Providing oxygen and nutrients and getting rid of waste

    Ⓓ Informing the brain when the skin makes contact with another surface

Paragraph 2 is marked with an arrow [→].

7. The word conserve in the passage is closest in meaning to

    Ⓐ notice   Ⓑ keep

    Ⓒ reuse   Ⓓ produce

8. According to paragraph 3, which of the following is true of the subcutaneous layer?

    Ⓐ It is mainly made up of fat.

    Ⓑ It does not have hair follicles.

    Ⓒ It is thicker than the other layers of skin.

    Ⓓ It contains the glands that keep the skin moist.

Paragraph 3 is marked with an arrow [→].

9. Look at the four squares [■] that indicate where the following sentence could be added to the passage.

    Therefore, parts of the body that commonly come in contact with other surfaces, such as fingertips, contain more nerve endings.

Where would the sentence best fit?

Click on a square [■] to add the sentence to the passage.

10. Directions: Complete the table by matching the phrases below. Select the appropriate phrases from the answer choices and match them to the layer of skin to which they relate. TWO of the answer choices will NOT be used.

Drag your answer choices to the spaces where they belong. To remove an answer choice, click on it. To review the passage, click on **View Text**.

Answer Choices	Epidermis layer
Ⓐ Is sometimes called the hypodermis	▶
Ⓑ Contains oil glands	**Dermis layer**
Ⓒ Is 1 mm thick on average	▶
Ⓓ Is the thickest layer of skin	▶
Ⓔ Protects the body from shock	
Ⓕ Contains Langerhans' cells to defend the body against invading substances	**Subcutaneous layer**
Ⓖ Is only present in places that need extra protection	▶
	▶

PART

Making
Inference

UNIT
05

Inference

■ Inference questions ask you about information that is suggested but not directly stated in the passage.

QUESTION TYPES

• From the passage, it can be inferred that

• What can be inferred from paragraph _ about X?

BASIC DRILLS 01

Fossils can form in different ways, but one of the most interesting ways is the process through which cast fossils are made. For any creature to be turned into a cast fossil, it must go through several stages. First, the creature must die and fall into a place where it can be preserved for a long time. The ideal location is a riverbed or ocean floor because there is a constant buildup of sediments such as mud or 5 sand. These sediments provide a protective cover for the dead creature, preventing other animals from eating it. They also reduce the effects of waves on its body. Later, layers of sediment begin to pile up, and pressure turns them to rock. Eventually, the creature's body decays and its original shape is preserved in the hole left by the fossilization process. Finally, as groundwater rich in minerals enters the rock and fills 10 the empty space, it hardens into the shape of the creature and forms a cast fossil.

1   What can be inferred from the passage about the dead creatures?
   Ⓐ They need warm temperatures to change into a cast fossil.
   Ⓑ Large-sized creatures are more commonly turned into cast fossils.
   Ⓒ They are preserved better when they are covered by mud instead of sand.
   Ⓓ Animals living in water are more likely to turn into cast fossils than land animals.

2   What can be inferred from the passage about cast fossils?
   Ⓐ Their size is usually larger than the original creature.
   Ⓑ Their composition is different from the original creature.
   Ⓒ They are only found in areas where water pressure is higher than normal.
   Ⓓ They have various types according to the places where they were formed.

BASIC DRILLS 02

*Altitude sickness is a condition sometimes experienced by people when they travel to high places. At high altitudes, air is thinner than at sea level, so there is less oxygen available. Because of the lack of oxygen, some people feel ill until their bodies adjust to the altitude. Altitude sickness may occur from 2,500 meters, and generally becomes more serious above 3,500 meters. 5

People suffering from altitude sickness may experience headaches, dizziness, stomachaches, and tiredness. The symptoms usually disappear within a day or two after a person ascends to a high altitude. In rare circumstances, altitude sickness may 10 result in a buildup of fluid in the lungs or brain. This condition can be quite serious and may even lead to death. The key to avoiding altitude sickness is giving the body time to adjust. A person is less likely to experience altitude sickness if he or she travels to a high altitude slowly, so the body can get used to the low-oxygen environment.

altitude: distance above sea level

1 From paragraph 2, it can be inferred that
   (A) fluid buildup in the lungs and brain usually occurs above 3,500 meters
   (B) some people suffer from altitude sickness without experiencing symptoms
   (C) altitude sickness is more closely related to the speed of upward movement than altitude
   (D) people who climb mountains slowly do not experience altitude sickness

2 What can be inferred from the passage about altitude sickness?
   (A) It affects everyone who travels to altitudes above 2,500 meters.
   (B) It is more likely to occur in people who have experienced it before.
   (C) Many people never get used to low-oxygen environments at high altitudes.
   (D) When symptoms disappear, it means the body has adapted to the altitude.

Underground Railroad: A Secret Network

The practice of slavery was common throughout the early United States. In the South, where conditions were especially harsh, black slaves were forced to work on large plantations and were not paid for their labor. Many Americans, however, felt that slavery should be abolished. The bravest of these people were part of a secret network known as the Underground Railroad. From the late eighteenth century to the end of slavery in 1865, they helped slaves escape from the plantations and travel to the northern U.S. or Canada, where slavery had been outlawed.

➡ All kinds of people participated in the Underground Railroad. ■ They provided transportation, food, money, and hiding places for the slaves. ■ Railroad terms were used to describe the system they created. ■ The houses and other places where slaves stayed were called "stations." ■ The people who guided the slaves along their journey were known as "conductors," and the slaves were often referred to as "passengers."

Everyone who took part in the Underground Railroad, including the slaves themselves, took great risks. If caught, they could be fined, jailed, or even killed. But through their bravery, the Underground Railroad succeeded in transporting a large number of slaves to freedom. It is estimated that 100,000 slaves were able to escape the South between 1810 and 1850 through the Underground Railroad.

1 Look at the four squares [■] that indicate where the following sentence could be added to the passage.

> Most were free blacks, but many whites were involved, as were some Native Americans.

Where would the sentence best fit?

2   What can be inferred from paragraph 2 about the Underground Railroad?

Ⓐ Most people involved were from the northern U.S.

Ⓑ Trains were often used in transporting slaves.

Ⓒ The use of railroad terms was a way to keep operations secret.

Ⓓ It took a very long time for slaves to succeed in escaping.

Paragraph 2 is marked with an arrow [➞].

3   Why does the author mention 100,000 slaves?

Ⓐ To show how many slaves were caught trying to escape

Ⓑ To demonstrate the success of the Underground Railroad

Ⓒ To explain how life in the South changed after the end of slavery

Ⓓ To emphasize the dangers faced by members of the Underground Railroad

4   From the passage, it can be inferred that the southern U.S.

Ⓐ had stricter laws than the northern U.S.

Ⓑ contained a larger population of freed slaves than other areas

Ⓒ practiced slavery longer than the northern U.S.

Ⓓ imported farm products from the northern U.S. and Canada

🗐 SUMMARY

Slavery was common in early America. Many Americans, however, were against _____,
and some of these people started the _____ _____. From the late eighteenth
century until 1865, this network helped slaves _____ the American South to the
northern U.S. or Canada. It provided _____, food, and money for slaves, hiding them
in safe places. The Underground Railroad was operated at great risk, but it helped about
_____ slaves escape to freedom.

Fireflies

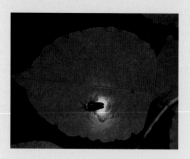

→ Fireflies are small, winged insects that have the ability to glow. In spite of their name, they are not flies but are actually a kind of beetle. There are about 200 firefly species found in *temperate and tropical environments around the world. Because they enjoy warm and humid ⁵ environments, they can be found in large numbers near streams and marshes.

→ Fireflies are interesting insects because they glow. They have light organs on the underside of their bodies. The organs light up in a series of flashes when they want to communicate. For the most part, fireflies use their blinking lights for mating. ¹⁰ For example, some species of male fireflies flash a pattern of signals to attract a female. To signal her interest, the female will flash back. They exchange flashes until they come together and mate. In addition, the females of some species of fireflies use their flashes to attract the males of other species as prey. By copying the mating flashes of other species of fireflies, they trick males and eat them. Another reason why ¹⁵ fireflies glow is to warn predators. The chemical that makes fireflies glow has a very unpleasant taste. Therefore, predators quickly learn to avoid these insects as a source of food.

*temperate: having mild weather, neither hot nor cold

1 According to paragraph 1, which of the following is true about fireflies?
  Ⓐ They belong to the beetle family.
  Ⓑ Their appearance is very similar to that of flies.
  Ⓒ They can be found in both dry and wet climates.
  Ⓓ There are only a few species of fireflies in the world.
  Paragraph 1 is marked with an arrow [→].

2   What can be inferred from paragraph 2 about the glowing of fireflies?

     Ⓐ It is brighter during the mating season.

     Ⓑ Only a few of their flash patterns are known.

     Ⓒ Each species of firefly has its own flash pattern for mating.

     Ⓓ Fireflies use a chemical that is also used by other glowing animals.

     Paragraph 2 is marked with an arrow [➡].

3   According to paragraph 2, the glowing of fireflies discourages predators because

     Ⓐ it leads them to other predators

     Ⓑ it is so bright that it frightens them away

     Ⓒ it makes fireflies seem larger than they are

     Ⓓ it is produced by a substance with a bad taste

     Paragraph 2 is marked with an arrow [➡].

4   What can be inferred from the passage about fireflies?

     Ⓐ Each species prefers a different habitat.

     Ⓑ Males usually glow more brightly than females.

     Ⓒ Light organs of both males and females work when they mate.

     Ⓓ They are sensitive to changes in their environments.

🗐 ORGANIZATION

- Fireflies
  - members of the _____ family
  - prefer warm and _____ climates, especially _____ and marshes
- The glowing of fireflies
  - fireflies have a(n) _____ organ on the underside of their bodies
  - is used to attract a mate or to eat other species of fireflies
  - warns off _____, as it has an unpleasant taste

Homo Erectus

➡ *Homo erectus* means "upright man" in Latin, and refers to a species of human that lived in Africa between 1.6 million and 250,000 years ago. As the Latin suggests, *Homo erectus* stood and walked upright like modern humans. In addition to walking, *Homo erectus* resembled modern humans in other ways, such as height, jaw shape and teeth. However, the *skulls of *Homo erectus* were only two-thirds the size of 5 modern human skulls, and they did not have the ability to make the complex sounds of modern speech.

Homo erectus were also different from their ancestors in many ways. It is believed that they were probably the first human species to hunt on a large-scale. ■ To do so, they developed more diverse and complicated tools such as hand axes, knives, and 10 clubs. ■ Perhaps most importantly, they were the first species to discover fire and used it for various purposes such as cooking and keeping warm. ■ They also used clothing made from animal skins to protect themselves from extreme weather conditions. ■ The *Homo erectus* species was also the first to leave Africa and move to other continents such as Asia and Europe. It is thought that they did this on foot in order to search for 15 food or to escape changes in climate.

*skull: the bones that make up the head

1 According to paragraph 1, which of the following is NOT a similarity between *Homo erectus* and modern humans?

Ⓐ Their height

Ⓑ Their style of walking

Ⓒ The size of their skulls

Ⓓ The shape of their teeth

Paragraph 1 is marked with an arrow [➡].

2   What can be inferred from paragraph 1 about *Homo erectus*?

    Ⓐ They lived in groups.

    Ⓑ They had at least basic communication skills.

    Ⓒ They walked faster than their earlier relatives.

    Ⓓ They were not as good at hunting as their ancestors.

    Paragraph 1 is marked with an arrow [➡].

3   Look at the four squares [■] that indicate where the following sentence could be added to the passage.

    They were made from stone and wood and allowed *Homo erectus* to hunt and kill animals like mammoths.

    Where would the sentence best fit?

4   What can be inferred from the passage about early humans?

    Ⓐ The earliest traveled to Africa on foot.

    Ⓑ Some species originally came from Asia and Europe.

    Ⓒ *Homo erectus* was not the first species that lived in Africa.

    Ⓓ *Homo erectus* was the last species before modern humans appeared.

SUMMARY

Homo erectus was a species of human ancestors living in _____ from about 1.6 million to 250,000 years ago. They walked _____ and looked similar to modern humans, but their _____ were only two thirds as big, and they couldn't produce complex speech. However, they created _____ to hunt with, such as axes and knives. They also discovered _____ and made clothing from animal skins. In addition, *Homo erectus* was the first human species to leave Africa for Asia and Europe.

Earth's Water Cycle

There is water all over the Earth: in oceans, lakes, rivers, and even under the ground. Yet no matter where it is, water is constantly moving. It travels from Earth's surface up into the atmosphere and back down again. This is a process called the water cycle, and it is driven by heat from the sun.

As the sun shines on Earth's streams, lakes, and seas, it heats up the water, and once the water reaches a certain temperature, it changes from a liquid to a gas called water vapor. The water vapor rises high into the atmosphere. This stage of the water cycle is known as evaporation.

→ The next stage is called condensation. It occurs when the temperature of the water vapor begins to drop due to the cooler air of the surrounding atmosphere. The gas changes back into a liquid, forming tiny water droplets. These droplets are so small that they are kept up in the air by winds. They stick together and form clouds. As more and more water droplets join together, they grow larger and heavier. Finally, they become heavy enough to fall back to Earth in the form of rain, snow, or hail.

Returning to Earth's surface, some of the water is absorbed into the ground. Much of it, though, flows across the surface until it finds its way into a river, lake, or ocean. This can take centuries or only minutes, depending on the landscape where it falls. But eventually, the sun's heat will cause it to evaporate once more, and the whole cycle will begin again.

5

10

15

20

1. Which of the sentences below best expresses the essential information in the highlighted sentence in the passage? *Incorrect* choices change the meaning in important ways or leave out essential information.

   (A) The liquid form of water can be changed to a gas if heat is applied.

   (B) Streams, lakes, and seas lose a lot of their water because of the sun.

   (C) Water becomes water vapor after it is heated to a certain point by the sun.

   (D) The sun heats up Earth's streams and lakes until the water reaches a desired temperature.

2. According to paragraph 3, when does water vapor become water droplets?

   (A) When it begins to fall back towards Earth

   (B) When it meets other water vapor in the air

   (C) When it is blown around by winds

   (D) When it enters a cooler area of the atmosphere

   Paragraph 3 is marked with an arrow [→].

3. The word it in the passage refers to

   (A) water   (B) surface

   (C) landscape   (D) the sun's heat

4. According to the passage, what can be inferred about the water cycle?

   (A) Without the sun, the cycle would not be possible.

   (B) It is responsible for creating Earth's oceans.

   (C) The cycle is faster in winter than in summer.

   (D) It has been going on ever since Earth was formed.

5. **Directions:** An introductory sentence for a brief summary of the passage is provided below. Complete the summary by selecting the THREE answer choices that express the most important ideas in the passage. Some sentences do not belong in the summary because they express ideas that are not presented in the passage or are minor ideas in the passage.

> Earth's water is constantly moving through a process known as the water cycle.
>
> •
>
> •
>
> •

Answer Choices

Ⓐ Water on the surface evaporates due to the sun's heat and rises high into the air.

Ⓑ Because water vapor is light, it drifts into the atmosphere.

Ⓒ After the water vapor cools back into a liquid, it forms clouds and then returns to the surface.

Ⓓ The rain, snow, or hail that falls from the sky is the result of the condensation stage of the water cycle.

Ⓔ Condensation occurs when the temperature of the air changes.

Ⓕ No matter where the water lands, it will eventually evaporate again as the cycle continues.

Vocabulary Review

A Choose the correct word for each definition.

> (A) ideal   (B) symptom   (C) estimate
>
> (D) marsh   (E) fossil   (F) jail

1. considered to be perfect: _____
2. to put someone in a prison: _____
3. an area of land that is always wet and soft: _____
4. a change in the body caused by a disease: _____
5. to make a guess about the quantity or value of something: _____

B Choose the best synonym for each pair of words or phrases.

> (A) similarity   (B) frighten   (C) originally
>
> (D) constantly   (E) preserve   (F) ascend

1. resemblance   likeness : _____
2. scare   alarm   : _____
3. climb   go up   : _____
4. continuously   nonstop   : _____

C Fill in the blanks with the best answer.

> chemicals   appeared   ax   continents   driven

1. My grandfather bought a new _____ to cut down trees.
2. Two ships suddenly _____ out of the darkness.
3. These _____ are used to kill harmful insects.
4. The movement is _____ by the need to protect the environment.

D Choose the word that is closest in meaning to each highlighted word.

1. It's going to be hot and humid next week.
   - (A) cloudy
   - (B) clear
   - (C) wet
   - (D) foggy

2. He told me not to reveal his secret under any circumstance.
   - (A) situation
   - (B) danger
   - (C) opinion
   - (D) place

3. Some people think that the death penalty should be abolished.
   - (A) established
   - (B) maintained
   - (C) changed
   - (D) ended

4. People in the meeting expressed diverse opinions about the issue.
   - (A) similar
   - (B) various
   - (C) reasonable
   - (D) serious

E Choose the opposite meaning of each highlighted word.

1. The hot material will harden as it cools.
   - (A) soften
   - (B) increase
   - (C) strengthen
   - (D) reduce

2. The ancient language was so complex that it took years to translate.
   - (A) common
   - (B) simple
   - (C) familiar
   - (D) boring

3. The animals moved due to the extreme weather conditions of the region.
   - (A) cold
   - (B) changeable
   - (C) regular
   - (D) mild

F Choose the correct phrase to complete each sentence.

1. He (depended on / participated in) the marathon with his friends.
2. It took me a while to (bring about / get used to) my new glasses.
3. The shipping company (is responsible for / brings up) the oil spill.

UNIT

Rhetorical Purpose

■ Rhetorical Purpose questions ask why the author includes certain information in the passage.

Glaciers are huge bodies of ice that travel slowly over land in polar regions and high mountain valleys. In places like these, the snow never melts away entirely, not even in the summer. Each year, the remaining snow piles up in layers. Over time, these layers build 5 up and their weight increases. This makes snow crystals beneath the surface press together and form small, hard balls. At depths of about 50 meters, increased weight causes these balls of snow to press together even more. This process results in the formation of ice crystals. These ice crystals combine to create glaciers that range from 90 to 3,000 meters in depth. As time goes by, 10 glaciers become dense and heavy. Because of the pressure of ice from above and the heat from the earth itself, the base of glaciers begins to melt. This provides a slippery surface that allows glaciers to slide down.

1 Why does the author mention about 50 meters?

Ⓐ To describe the average thickness of glaciers

Ⓑ To explain how much glaciers move during a year

Ⓒ To introduce where the change of snow into ice crystals happens

Ⓓ To indicate how many layers of snowfall typically build up during a year

2 The author mentions heat from the earth in order to

Ⓐ compare the temperature of glaciers around the world

Ⓑ point out that glaciers are limited in size by certain factors

Ⓒ describe why there are fewer glaciers now than ever before

Ⓓ explain the factor that causes the sliding movement of glaciers

BASIC DRILLS 02

Palm oil is one of the most popular plant oils in the world. It comes from the fruit of the oil palm tree, *Elaeis guineensis*. The majority of the oil comes from Southeast Asia. It doesn't spoil or burn easily and is cheaper than other edible oils. Because of this, it is widely used as a cooking oil in Asia. It is also used in foods, soaps, and skin products sold all over the world. 5

However, the low price of palm oil hides a high environmental cost in the countries where it is produced. Farmers are burning acres of swamp forests to make room for more oil palms. The fires fill the air with smoke and kill the forest. It causes wild orangutans and Sumatran tigers to lose their homes and become endangered. Furthermore, since swamp forests hold large amounts of carbon dioxide and methane, 10 these greenhouse gases escape into the air when the forests die. Huge amounts of methane are also given off by oil processing, so the production of palm oil speeds up climate change.

1 The author mentions that the low price of palm oil hides a high environmental cost in order to
Ⓐ correct a misunderstanding about the cheap price of palm oil
Ⓑ stress the negative sides of palm oil despite its benefits
Ⓒ demonstrate that burning forests doesn't create profit
Ⓓ explain why so many farmers want to grow oil palms

2 Why does the author mention wild orangutans and Sumatran tigers?
Ⓐ To criticize hunting practices in swamp forests
Ⓑ To provide information about animals who eat oil palms
Ⓒ To explain why certain animals are more sensitive to smoke
Ⓓ To give examples of animals in danger due to the loss of swamp forests

John James Audubon

John James Audubon was a nineteenth-century American naturalist and painter. He is famous for his remarkable book *Birds of America*, which contains hundreds of hand-drawn images of North American birds.

Audubon was born on April 26, 1785, in Haiti. He came to the United States at the age of eighteen to avoid being sent to fight in the Napoleonic Wars. While Audubon 5 was living in Pennsylvania, he was surrounded by nature. He spent much of his time outdoors hunting, fishing, and drawing. He was especially interested in birds, so he started painting them as realistically as possible and studying their habits. Eventually, his hobby turned into an ambitious goal: to catalog and paint all of the bird species in North America. He began traveling around the country, observing birds and painting 10 them. To make his work more realistic, he sometimes hired hunters to bring him bodies of birds to study in detail.

Audubon's project grew into a dream of putting together his collection of bird paintings as a book. Finally, *Birds of America* was published in 1838, with 435 paintings of birds accompanied by descriptive text. During its time, *Birds of America* 15 was a great success. Even today, it is still regarded as one of the finest picture books ever printed.

1   **Why does the author mention the Napoleonic Wars?**

        Ⓐ To explain why Audubon traveled to the United States

        Ⓑ To indicate how Audubon first became interested in birds

        Ⓒ To describe how Audubon was influenced by surrounding nature

        Ⓓ To suggest that it was difficult to study nature in France at that time

2 The author mentions hunters in order to

   (A) suggest that Audubon met people from various fields

   (B) describe the people who guided Audubon on his outdoor trips

   (C) explain how Audubon could draw birds so realistically

   (D) give an example of people who supported his idea for a book

3 Which of the sentences below best expresses the essential information in the highlighted sentence in the passage?

   (A) Audubon's collection of bird images and descriptions was published in 1838.

   (B) Audubon wrote descriptions of all the birds in his paintings.

   (C) Audubon published *Birds of America* as well as a series of paintings of birds.

   (D) *Birds of America* is famous for its detailed explanations of 435 birds.

4 According to the passage, which of the following is true about the life of Audubon?

   (A) He started painting birds to earn a living.

   (B) He received little recognition for his book during his lifetime.

   (C) He studied birds in Haiti before he moved to America.

   (D) He lived in an environment where he could experience nature.

SUMMARY

John James Audubon was a naturalist and painter in the 19th century. He came to the United States and lived in Pennsylvania, surrounded by _____. He developed an interest in _____, making realistic paintings and studying their habits. Eventually, he decided to _____ and paint every species of bird in North America. His project resulted in the book, _____ _____ _____, which featured 435 drawings and descriptions of birds.

Eruption of Mount St. Helens

In Washington State in America, there is an *active volcano called Mount St. Helens. It is responsible for the most destructive eruption in the history of the United States, which occurred on May 18, 1980.

The volcano produced its first warning sign on March 20, in the form of an earthquake. A week later, a minor explosion made a hole in the mountain and threw ash and steam into the air. For the next month, similar small explosions occurred periodically. Finally, on May 18, immediately after another earthquake, the volcano suddenly erupted. Hot ash burst out of the volcano and traveled upward to a height of ten miles. A large amount of mud started to slide down the mountain and covered everything it touched–houses, roads, bridges, and railroads.

Nearly every form of life that was within 320 square kilometers of Mount St. Helens was killed during the violent eruption. In all, 57 people and several thousand animals, including deer and bears, lost their lives. Moreover, the Toutle River Valley was flooded with mud that reached a depth of almost 50 meters.

active volcano: a volcano that has erupted recently and will probably erupt in the future

1 The word periodically in the passage is closest in meaning to

  Ⓐ daily   Ⓑ seriously

  Ⓒ suddenly   Ⓓ occasionally

2   The word it in the passage refers to
(A) ash
(B) earthquake
(C) mud
(D) mountain

3   The author mentions the Toutle River Valley in order to
(A) show the location where the most animals were killed
(B) describe what the mountain was like before the eruption
(C) give an example of the destruction caused by the volcano
(D) suggest that the eruption came as a surprise to many people

4   How does the author explain the eruption of Mount St. Helens?
(A) By comparing it to other eruptions throughout history
(B) By presenting the causes and effects of the eruption
(C) By summarizing the events before the eruption and its impact
(D) By listing all of the earthquakes that occurred before the eruption

SUMMARY

Mount St. Helens, an active _____ in Washington State, was responsible for the most destructive eruption in U.S. history. It occurred on May 18, 1980. The first warning sign was a(n) _____ on March 20, followed by minor explosions. Finally the volcano erupted. Hot _____ flew into the air and a giant mud slide swept down the mountain. The result was the deaths of 57 people and thousands of _____.

The Attribution Theory

Attribution theory is an area of social psychology that describes how we explain human behavior. According to this theory, whenever we make judgments about the causes of a person's behavior, these judgments are guided by both internal and external factors. Internal factors involve the personality or inner nature of a person. External factors, on the other hand, refer to situational details that are out of the person's control, like the weather.

→ The theory suggests that there are two basic problems with how we explain people's behavior, and that these problems lead to inaccurate judgments. The first is called the fundamental attribution error. It says we tend to explain another person's behavior by focusing only on internal factors. In other words, we see the behavior as the result of the person's character. For example, if a man yells at you, you will probably think he is a mean person. But in fact, he may simply have had a stressful day at work.

→ The other problem is related to how we view our own behavior. It is called the self-serving bias. When we succeed at something, we think it is because of our skill. But when we fail, we are more likely to see it as bad luck or blame someone else for causing it. Therefore, according to the self-serving bias, we focus too much on internal factors when we succeed and external factors when we fail.

1   Which of the sentences below best expresses the essential information in the highlighted sentence in the passage?

Ⓐ Both internal and external factors influence our judgments about the causes of people's behavior.

Ⓑ We are often interested in the reasons for other people's behavior.

Ⓒ The theory suggests our behavior is heavily influenced by other people's judgments.

Ⓓ We make judgments about people based on external factors rather than internal ones.

2 Why does the author mention a ==stressful day at work==?

   Ⓐ To show how a person's character causes certain behaviors

   Ⓑ To give an example of an external factor that can influence behavior

   Ⓒ To explain when the fundamental attribution error commonly occurs

   Ⓓ To prove how internal and external factors never work together

3 According to paragraph 2, what happens when people make a judgment about the behavior of others?

   Ⓐ They forget about internal factors.

   Ⓑ They try to avoid attribution errors.

   Ⓒ They focus on their own personalities.

   Ⓓ They ignore possible external factors.

   Paragraph 2 is marked with an arrow [➡].

4 In paragraph 3, the author discusses success and failure in order to

   Ⓐ describe a common external factor

   Ⓑ show that the self-serving bias changes how others see us

   Ⓒ indicate how the self-serving bias affects our judgments about ourselves

   Ⓓ suggest that people focus on external factors to explain their own behavior

   Paragraph 3 is marked with an arrow [➡].

ORGANIZATION

- Attribution theory
  - describes how humans make judgments about the _____ of behavior
  - these judgments are influenced by internal and _____ factors
- **Fundamental attribution error**: a tendency to inaccurately judge the behavior of others
  - judgments are based on _____ factors without considering _____ factors
- **Self-serving bias**: a cause of inaccurate judgments about our own behavior
  - when we _____, we put too much emphasis on internal factors
  - when we _____, we put too much emphasis on external factors

The Dangers of Algal Blooms

Algae are tiny, single-celled plant-like organisms that live in freshwater and ocean environments. They are an important source of food for many animals. Sometimes, algae populations grow rapidly and large numbers of them come together and float at the surface. These large groups of algae are known as algal blooms. Blooms can appear in different colors, such as green, brown, or red. The   5 colors depend on which algae species they are made of.

Various changes in water conditions foster the growth of a bloom. For example, unusually warm water can cause a bloom to form. An increase in the nutrients that algae eat has the same effect. Such nutrients include phosphorus and nitrogen, which are often found in man-made pollution. Because of this, water pollution can   10 lead to the growth of an algal bloom.

Algal blooms can have a variety of negative effects on plant and animal life. Most commonly, the algae in a bloom create a thick cloud that keeps sunlight from reaching the plants and fish that live underwater. In addition, the algae use up much of the water's oxygen as they grow. Sometimes there is not enough left for   15 other plants and animals.

Yet there is an even more dangerous threat from algal blooms. Some algae species produce small amounts of toxins–harmful chemicals. Because there are so many algae in a bloom, the toxin levels in the surrounding water are quite high. Toxic algal blooms often kill large numbers of fish and other wildlife. Even humans   20 can be affected if they eat fish that have been poisoned.

TOEFL Reading

1. Why does the author discuss algae species?

      Ⓐ To introduce different shapes of algal blooms

      Ⓑ To explain what determines the color of algal blooms

      Ⓒ To show why animals depend on algae for food

      Ⓓ To describe the environments where algal blooms happen

2. The word foster in the passage is closest in meaning to

      Ⓐ prevent

      Ⓑ maintain

      Ⓒ restrain

      Ⓓ encourage

3. Why does the author mention water pollution?

      Ⓐ To explain one cause of algal blooms

      Ⓑ To describe how bodies of water can be heated

      Ⓒ To show why humans should clean up algal blooms

      Ⓓ To identify the most important result of algal blooms

4. Which of the sentences below best expresses the essential information in the highlighted sentence in the passage? *Incorrect* choices change the meaning in important ways or leave out essential information.

      Ⓐ Without a certain amount of light, plants and fish cannot live in water.

      Ⓑ The thickness of an algal bloom depends on how much sunlight it receives.

      Ⓒ Because so many algae gather in a bloom, they create a thick cloud.

      Ⓓ Underwater species cannot get enough sunlight because of thick algal blooms.

5. **Directions:** An introductory sentence for a brief summary of the passage is provided below. Complete the summary by selecting the THREE answer choices that express the most important ideas in the passage. Some sentences do not belong in the summary because they express ideas that are not presented in the passage or are minor ideas in the passage.

> When large numbers of algae join together, they create an algal bloom.
>
> •
>
> •
>
> •

Answer Choices

Ⓐ Algae in a bloom compete with the underwater plants and fish for sunlight.

Ⓑ Increases in temperature and nutrients in the water cause the formation of algal blooms.

Ⓒ In order to stop algal blooms from appearing, people must limit levels of water pollution.

Ⓓ Algal blooms harm wildlife by blocking sunlight and using up much of the oxygen in the water.

Ⓔ Some types of algal blooms create a poison that can kill plants and animals and even affect humans.

Ⓕ Phosphorus and nitrogen are two sources of the increase in algae populations.

Vocabulary Review

A Choose the correct word for each definition.

Ⓐ blame	Ⓑ catalog	Ⓒ foster
Ⓓ surround	Ⓔ ash	Ⓕ range

1. to make a list of: _____

2. to exist within two particular limits: _____

3. to be all around something: _____

4. to promote the development of something: _____

5. the material which remains when something burns: _____

B Choose the best synonym for each pair of words or phrases.

Ⓐ entirely	Ⓑ slippery	Ⓒ burst
Ⓓ ambitious	Ⓔ threat	Ⓕ occur

1. explode   blow up   : _____

2. danger   risk   : _____

3. happen   take place : _____

4. totally   completely : _____

C Fill in the blanks with the best answer.

yelled	combine	earthquake	judgment	accompanied

1. I _____ through the noise of the crowd to get my friend's attention.

2. A powerful _____ hit the town early in the morning.

3. Don't make a(n) _____ about the movie before you watch.

4. The first step to making my favorite dessert is to _____ chocolate and milk.

D Choose the word that is closest in meaning to each highlighted word.

1. Many external forces influence the way we behave.
   - (A) powerful
   - (B) outside
   - (C) basic
   - (D) unknown

2. The wild mushroom is not edible because it is poisonous.
   - (A) popular
   - (B) nutritious
   - (C) eatable
   - (D) colorful

3. Surprisingly, Sam handled the problem immediately without any help.
   - (A) exactly
   - (B) completely
   - (C) instantly
   - (D) easily

4. The teacher was observing how the children played together.
   - (A) watching
   - (B) reporting
   - (C) wondering
   - (D) guessing

E Choose the opposite meaning of each highlighted word.

1. We need additional data because the first set was inaccurate.
   - (A) important
   - (B) helpful
   - (C) exact
   - (D) humorous

2. It is difficult to ignore my boss's opinion about the project.
   - (A) check up on
   - (B) look after
   - (C) come up with
   - (D) pay attention to

3. The factories are not allowed to dump toxic waste into the river.
   - (A) light
   - (B) useful
   - (C) common
   - (D) harmless

F Choose the correct phrase to complete each sentence.

1. A lot of fallen leaves (passed out / piled up) on the street.
2. In the woods, I saw a snake (slide down / put off) into a hole.
3. The English language is (related to / known as) the German language.

Actual Practice Test

ACTUAL PRACTICE TEST 2

Ancient Athens and Sparta

Ancient Greece was different from many modern countries. Instead of a single national government, the Greeks had hundreds of self-governed city-states. Together, these city-states formed a collection of small republics that shared a religion and a language. However, in spite of their common heritage, each Greek city-state was unique. They made their own laws and had their own customs. Two of the most famous Greek city-states were Athens and Sparta.

→ Athens, the largest of the city-states, was located in southern Greece, near the sea and surrounded by rivers. Life in Athens was centered on culture and education. Many famous Greek artists, writers, and philosophers came from Athens, including Socrates, Plato, and Phidias. ■ Additionally, Athenians practiced an early form of democracy. ■ The crucial body in their government was a group called the assembly. ■ Large meetings of the assembly were held on a slope of a hill in Athens. ■ In these meetings, people could vote on important issues. However, women, foreigners, and slaves had no voting rights. Athenian women, no matter what their class, were denied freedom and were controlled by their father or husband. They could not receive an education or participate in business affairs.

Sparta was also located in southern Greece, on plains surrounded by mountains. Spartan society was very different from Athenian society. Instead of culture and art, it focused mainly on military strength, so Spartans spent much of their lives training and fighting. This was possible because they had slaves, known as Helots, to farm their land. Physical fitness was very important for both men and women. Although women did not participate in wars, they trained for physical fitness. The city-state of Sparta had a complicated government, where most of the power was in the hands of a few. In one sense, it was a monarchy led by two kings. However, the kings shared their power with two groups of elected officials: the gerousia and the ephors. The gerousia was a council of twenty-eight elders and two kings, and the ephors were five citizens. As in Athens, Spartan women did not have voting rights. However, they were permitted other freedoms, such as receiving an education and owning property.

1. The word heritage in the passage is closest in meaning to

    Ⓐ tradition

    Ⓑ similarity

    Ⓒ friendship

    Ⓓ characteristic

2. The author mentions Socrates, Plato, and Phidias in order to

    Ⓐ prove that Athens was the largest city-state

    Ⓑ suggest that many people know about famous ancient Greeks

    Ⓒ support the idea that Athens focused on culture and education

    Ⓓ give examples of people who influenced the life of the Greeks

3. The word affairs in the passage is closest in meaning to

    Ⓐ matters

    Ⓑ meetings

    Ⓒ challenges

    Ⓓ discussions

4. According to paragraph 2, which of the following is true about the government of Athens?

    Ⓐ It had a king or a queen.

    Ⓑ It allowed women to own land.

    Ⓒ It focused on the expansion of the country.

    Ⓓ It permitted some people to vote on state issues.

    Paragraph 2 is marked with an arrow [➡].

5. The word it in the passage refers to

   Ⓐ Greece   Ⓑ Spartan society

   Ⓒ Athenian society   Ⓓ art

6. Why does the author mention Helots?

   Ⓐ To show that Spartans were cruel to their slaves

   Ⓑ To suggest that agriculture was important to Spartans

   Ⓒ To point out that life in Sparta was similar to life in Athens

   Ⓓ To explain how Spartans managed to spend all their time training

7. Which of the sentences below best expresses the essential information in the highlighted sentence in the passage? *Incorrect* choices change the meaning in important ways or leave out essential information.

   Ⓐ Sparta was a city-state with a powerful government.

   Ⓑ Much of Sparta's power was divided up among its citizens.

   Ⓒ Sparta's complex government gave power to a small group of people.

   Ⓓ In Sparta, the government controlled only a small part of the population.

8. According to the passage, what is a similarity between Athens and Sparta?

   Ⓐ Women were not given the right to vote.

   Ⓑ People focused on increasing their physical strength.

   Ⓒ Decisions were made in a democratic way at meetings.

   Ⓓ A council of officials was chosen to share the power of a ruler.

9. Look at the four squares [■] that indicate where the following sentence could be added to the passage.

> Since they were open to citizens, it was possible for people to express their opinions about state decisions.

Where would the sentence best fit?

Click on a square [■] to add the sentence to the passage.

10. **Directions:** Complete the table by matching the phrases below. Select the appropriate phrases from the answer choices and match them to the Greek city-state to which they relate. TWO of the answer choices will NOT be used.

Drag your answer choices to the spaces where they belong. To remove an answer choice, click on it. To review the passage, click on **View Text**.

Answer Choices	Athens
Ⓐ Had a society that was interested in culture	▶
Ⓑ Was located in northern Greece	▶
Ⓒ Denied women access to education	▶
Ⓓ Considered physical fitness important	Sparta
Ⓔ Owned slaves known as Helots	▶
Ⓕ Held assembly meetings on a hill	▶
Ⓖ Forced women to participate in wars	

PART

Recognizing
Organization

UNIT

07

Insertion

■ Insertion questions ask you to choose where a given sentence fits best in the passage.

In ancient Egypt, the seasons were closely linked to the annual flooding of the Nile River. There were three seasons, and they were known as Akhet, Peret, and Shemu. Akhet was the season when the river flooded. It regularly occurred between June and September according to the modern calendar. **1A** Because the fields were underwater, people were unable to farm during this season. **1B** During the season called Peret, the floodwaters finally dried up. **1C** This season lasted from October to February and was typically cooler than the other two seasons. **1D** The drying of the floodwaters left behind a layer of rich soil along the banks of the Nile. It was perfectly suited for supporting crops. When the ground was firm enough to walk on, farmers prepared their fields and began planting seeds. **2A** The final season in ancient Egypt was Shemu, a dry period lasting from March to May. **2B** For farmers, this was a very busy season for harvesting their crops. **2C** It was also a time of preparation when people improved the canals before the upcoming flood. **2D**

1 Look at the four squares [■] that indicate where the following sentence could be added to the passage.

> What they did instead was to repair their equipment or spend their time fishing for extra food or money.

Where would the sentence best fit?

2 Look at the four squares [■] that indicate where the following sentence could be added to the passage.

> They had to safely store their crops ahead of the Nile's flooding cycle.

Where would the sentence best fit?

BASIC DRILLS 02

Many kinds of animals use special chemicals to send messages to other members of the same species. These chemicals are called pheromones. According to scientists, pheromones have a variety of purposes. As a result, they have been grouped into categories based on their function. **1A** These categories range from sex and trail pheromones to territorial pheromones. **1B** Among these, the most researched are ₅ probably sex pheromones. **1C** These chemicals are involved in mating practices and help animals attract mates, sometimes over great distances. **1D** A completely different use of pheromones can be found in some kinds of ants. They use trail pheromones to guide other ants from the nest to sources of food. **2A** Another use of pheromones is for claiming territory. **2B** Dogs often use territorial pheromones to mark their territory. ₁₀ **2C** They release these pheromones as they *urinate. **2D**

*urinate: to release liquid waste stored in the body

1 Look at the four squares [■] that indicate where the following sentence could be added to the passage.

> For example, the pheromones in some butterflies are able to attract a potential mate from up to ten kilometers away.

Where would the sentence best fit?

2 Look at the four squares [■] that indicate where the following sentence could be added to the passage.

> These pheromones will be continually updated until the food supply disappears.

Where would the sentence best fit?

The Roman Colosseum

The Colosseum in Rome is one of the most famous buildings in the world. Originally called the Flavian Amphitheater, it was named after the family of Vespasian and Titus, the two emperors who had it built. It was constructed from 72 AD and officially opened in the year 80 AD. ■ It measured 188 meters long and 156 meters wide, with a height of 48 meters. ■ It had four seating levels with 80 entrances. ■ The huge building could hold as many as 55,000 people. ■

The Colosseum, and the various events that took place in it, were a major attraction in Ancient Rome. Most of these events centered on death and destruction. These included animal fighting and wild animal hunts. Below the Colosseum, big cats, buffaloes, bears, and elephants were kept in cages. They were lifted from below into the *arena, where they were forced to fight each other. ■ However, these contests were not the main attraction of the shows. ■ The people in the Colosseum wanted to see gladiators—professional fighters, slaves, and prisoners of war—fight to the death. ■ When a fighter was badly hurt and wanted to quit, he would raise his index finger. ■ Upon seeing this, his sponsor—usually the emperor himself—would decide whether the wounded should be allowed to live or die. If the emperor gave a thumbs-up, it meant life and if he gave a thumbs-down, it meant death.

*arena: a large enclosed area where sports contests and entertainment take place

1 Which of the sentences below best expresses the essential information in the highlighted sentence in the passage?

Ⓐ Two emperors, Vespasian and Titus, chose the name for it.

Ⓑ The Vespasian family built the Flavian Amphitheater for two emperors.

Ⓒ It was the first building to be built in honor of Vespasian and Titus.

Ⓓ It was named the Flavian Amphitheater in honor of the family that constructed the building.

2   Look at the four squares [■] in paragraph 1 that indicate where the following sentence could be added to the passage.

On the first three floors, entrances were in the form of an arch, while the fourth floor had rectangular entrances.

Where would the sentence best fit?

3   Look at the four squares [■] in paragraph 2 that indicate where the following sentence could be added to the passage.

During the fights, gladiators wore armor and used nets, swords, and spears as weapons.

Where would the sentence best fit?

4   The word wounded is closest in meaning to
   Ⓐ weak   Ⓑ disabled
   Ⓒ injured   Ⓓ poor

📋 SUMMARY

The Colosseum in Rome, originally called the Flavian Amphitheater, opened in the year 80 AD. The huge building had _____ seating levels that could hold up to 55,000 people. Events held in the Colosseum included animal fights and large animal _____. However, the main attraction was the gladiators who would _____ to the death. If a gladiator wanted to quit, his _____ decided whether he lived or died.

The Invention of the Traffic Light

Before the twentieth century, traffic conditions were often chaotic and dangerous in many cities. In New York City, for example, various vehicles, horses, and *pedestrians all traveled on the same roads. There were few traffic regulations in place and no traffic signals. The need for signals became apparent, especially as automobiles became more common and accidents happened more often. 5

The world's first traffic signal system appeared in London in the late nineteenth century. ■ A railroad engineer named John Peake Knight created it by applying the signal system that had been used for railroads. ■ His system included colored posts that had to be operated manually by a traffic officer. ■ After some years, electricity allowed for traffic signals to become safer and more widespread. ■ The first recorded 10 electrical signal was designed in Salt Lake City and included a wooden box with painted red and green lights mounted on a pole. It was connected to the wire system used for trolley cars and had to be controlled by a police officer as well.

Traffic signal design was advanced further by an African-American inventor, Garrett Morgan. ■ As he saw there were still many accidents with the two-signal 15 lights, he added a "warning" yellow light to the old system. ■ But for more than thirty years, two-light signals were used in the streets of New York City. ■ They were finally replaced with the more modern red-yellow-green lights in the 1950s. ■ A three-light traffic system is now standard in modern cities.

pedestrian: a person who is walking, especially on a street near other vehicles

1 The word apparent in the passage is closest in meaning to
  (A) obvious
  (B) reasonable
  (C) complete
  (D) well-known

2 Look at the four squares [■] in paragraph 2 that indicate where the following sentence could be added to the passage.

At night, they were replaced with red and green lamps powered by gas.

Where would the sentence best fit?

3 Look at the four squares [■] in paragraph 3 that indicate where the following sentence could be added to the passage.

It was the first three-signal electrical traffic light system.

Where would the sentence best fit?

4 According to the passage, which of the following is NOT true about traffic lights?
Ⓐ The first traffic signal was installed in London.
Ⓑ The early traffic-signal systems needed to be hand-operated.
Ⓒ The first electrical traffic signal was designed after three-signal system was introduced.
Ⓓ The signals in New York used a two-light system for more than thirty years.

📖 SUMMARY

Before the twentieth century, various kinds of traffic in cities and a lack of signals made traffic conditions chaotic and _____. The first traffic signal was introduced in London, and it had _____ posts as well as gas lights. Later, _____ allowed for traffic signals to become safer and more widespread. Another important development in traffic signals was the inclusion of a _____ light, meant as a warning before the stop light. In modern cities, having three-color lights is standard.

Latitude and Longitude

Latitude and longitude are measurements that tell the location of something on the Earth's surface. They are a system of imaginary lines that cover the entire globe. Locations expressed in latitude and longitude are written in degrees and use the degree symbol(°).   5

→ On a map, latitude lines are horizontal lines that run in the same direction as the *equator. They are all the same distance from each other, with about 69 miles between each degree of latitude. ■ Starting with the equator, which marks zero degrees, lines of latitude are numbered from 0 to 90 degrees. ■ To distinguish between northern and southern *hemispheres, degrees of latitude in   10 the north are measured with positive numbers, and those in the south are measured with negative numbers. ■ For example, the North Pole represents 90 degrees and the South Pole represents -90 degrees. ■

→ On the other hand, longitude lines, sometimes called meridians, run vertically, passing through both poles. The meridian of Greenwich, England, marks zero degrees   15 in longitude. ■ For this reason, it is known as the prime meridian. ■ The eastern side of the prime meridian contains the positive numbers from 0 to 180, and the western side contains the negative numbers from 0 to -180. ■ A single line represents both 180 degrees and -180 degrees, and is located on the opposite side of the Earth from the prime meridian. ■   20

*equator: an imaginary line which is drawn around the middle of the Earth
*hemisphere: a half of the globe

1   Look at the four squares [■] in paragraph 2 that indicate where the following
     sentence could be added to the passage.

     Therefore, the line of latitude that represents 90 degrees is farthest from the
     equator.

     Where would the sentence best fit?

2 Look at the four squares [■] in paragraph 3 that indicate where the following sentence could be added to the passage.

> Like the equator, there are positive numbers on one side and negative numbers on the other side.

Where would the sentence best fit?

3 According to paragraphs 2 and 3, positive numbers and negative numbers are used in order to

Ⓐ divide north from south and east from west

Ⓑ distinguish lines of latitude from lines of longitude

Ⓒ explain the relationship between the equator and the prime meridian

Ⓓ compare the location of the equator to that of the prime meridian

Paragraphs 2 and 3 are marked with arrows [➡].

4 According to paragraph 3, which of the following is true of lines of longitude?

Ⓐ They all pass through Greenwich, England.

Ⓑ They run in the same direction as the equator.

Ⓒ Negative numbers are used for the eastern side of the prime meridian.

Ⓓ Negative 180 degrees and positive 180 degrees are the same line.

Paragraph 3 is marked with an arrow [➡].

🗀 **ORGANIZATION**

- Latitude and longitude – system of _____ used to locate points on the Earth's surface
- Lines of latitude
  - run horizontally from the _____ / numbered from 0 to 90 degrees
  - lines in the northern hemisphere use _____ numbers and those in the southern hemisphere use _____ numbers
- Lines of longitude
  - run _____ / numbered from 0 to _____ degrees
  - lines to the east of the prime meridian use positive numbers and those to the west use negative numbers

TOEFL Reading

Aestheticism

→ Aestheticism is a European arts movement of the late nineteenth century. It was founded on the principle that art exists only for the sake of beauty. The movement began in response to the general ugliness and lack of sophistication of the industrial age. Philosopher Immanuel Kant laid the foundations for aestheticism in the eighteenth century. He believed that art can exist solely as self-expression and does not need to provide a moral, religious, or political message.

→ At the time aestheticism began to appear, the values of Victorian culture were widely accepted. ■ The Victorians believed that art and literature had an obligation to promote moral values and behavior. ■ Aestheticism challenged this traditional idea. ■ The view of those involved in the movement is well-expressed in their motto, "art for art's sake." ■ Aesthetic painters used soft colors and simplified forms while avoiding the complex detail that Victorians preferred. These qualities were not only seen in visual art but were also reflected in the literature of the time. Charles Algernon Swinburne combined various poetic forms to express ideas that Victorians found immoral. Walter Pater wrote essays that praised Renaissance culture and the individualism of Renaissance artists. Among aesthetic writers, the most famous by far was Oscar Wilde. He avoided the Victorian preference for serious writing by expressing humor in his compositions.

→ By the late 1890s, however, many members of the British public openly mocked aestheticism for being foolish and empty. Many others began to see aesthetic artists as criminally immoral. The movement ended quickly in 1895 when Oscar Wilde was taken to prison. Nonetheless, the philosophy of "art for art's sake" continued to live on, and it influenced artists and the public well into the twentieth century.

TOEFL Reading

 VOLUME   HELP   OK   NEXT

1. The word moral in the passage is closest in meaning to

   Ⓐ instructive

   Ⓑ governmental

   Ⓒ commercial

   Ⓓ ethical

2. According to paragraphs 1 and 2, which of the following is NOT true of aestheticism?

   Ⓐ It regarded beauty as a quality that art should possess.

   Ⓑ It sought values that were different from those of Victorian culture.

   Ⓒ It encouraged people to behave in proper ways.

   Ⓓ It employed soft colors and basic forms in paintings.

   Paragraphs 1 and 2 are marked with arrows [➡].

3. What can be inferred from paragraph 3 about Oscar Wilde?

   Ⓐ He wanted to avoid public attention.

   Ⓑ He was an influential member of the artistic community.

   Ⓒ He was devoted to changing the British legal system.

   Ⓓ He spent the most of his life in prison.

   Paragraph 3 is marked with an arrow [➡].

4. Look at the four squares [■] that indicate where the following sentence could be added to the passage.

   Aesthetic artists pursued pure beauty and self-expression in art, instead.

   Where would the sentence best fit?

5. **Directions:** An introductory sentence for a brief summary of the passage is provided below. Complete the summary by selecting the THREE answer choices that express the most important ideas in the passage. Some sentences do not belong in the summary because they express ideas that are not presented in the passage or are minor ideas in the passage.

> Aestheticism was an artistic movement that existed in the late 1800s in Europe.
>
> •
>
> •
>
> •

Answer Choices

Ⓐ Aesthetic beliefs about art went against the typical Victorian view that art should convey a moral, religious, or political message.

Ⓑ People in the Victorian era were open to new ideas and expected artists to express themselves openly.

Ⓒ Aestheticism was based on the idea that art should exist only as an expression of beauty, as stated in the motto "art for art's sake."

Ⓓ Aesthetic artists rejected the concept of individualism and believed that artists should see themselves as members of a community.

Ⓔ The features of aestheticism were found in poems, essays, and other literary works as well as in visual art.

Ⓕ Oscar Wilde was sent to jail in 1895, but the aesthetic movement continued to influence artists and the public.

Vocabulary Review

A   Choose the correct word for each definition.

Ⓐ avoid	Ⓑ category	Ⓒ cage
Ⓓ praise	Ⓔ pursue	Ⓕ emperor

1. the ruler of an empire: _____

2. to stay away from something or someone: _____

3. to try to achieve something: _____

4. a group of things with a common feature: _____

5. a container with bars in which animals can be kept: _____

B   Choose the best synonym for each pair of words.

Ⓐ equipment	Ⓑ obligation	Ⓒ potential
Ⓓ regulation	Ⓔ firm	Ⓕ chemical

1. rule   law   : _____

2. hard   solid   : _____

3. possible   likely   : _____

4. duty   responsibility : _____

C   Fill in the blanks with the best answer.

distinguish	harvest	imaginary	chaotic	composition

1. The students learned the rules of _____ in their writing class.

2. The subway is completely _____ during rush hour.

3. Can you _____ her accent from that of other regions in the country?

4. She wrote a story about a(n) _____ boy and his fight against pirates.

D Choose the word that is closest in meaning to each highlighted word.

1. The song was mocked for its strange lyrics.
   - (A) ridiculed
   - (B) disliked
   - (C) discovered
   - (D) rejected

2. The annual technology conference is held every July.
   - (A) important
   - (B) international
   - (C) yearly
   - (D) private

3. The new concert hall can hold up to 20,000 people.
   - (A) support
   - (B) accommodate
   - (C) attract
   - (D) control

4. Because it is very dry, fires are frequent in spring.
   - (A) unique
   - (B) bright
   - (C) sensitive
   - (D) usual

E Choose the opposite meaning of each highlighted word.

1. I regularly visit my grandmother to see how she's doing.
   - (A) officially
   - (B) rarely
   - (C) often
   - (D) lately

2. The young soldier was wounded badly on the battlefield.
   - (A) tested
   - (B) healed
   - (C) saved
   - (D) accepted

3. There was actually negative population growth in this region last year.
   - (A) positive
   - (B) expected
   - (C) creative
   - (D) unknown

F Choose the correct phrase to complete each sentence.

1. We have to leave this area (in honor of / ahead of) the incoming hurricane.
2. Certain types of clouds are (linked to / anxious for) specific weather conditions.
3. We may or may not have a company picnic tomorrow, (depending on / resulting in) the weather.

UNIT

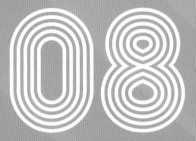

Prose Summary

- Prose Summary questions ask you to complete a summary of the passage by choosing the three sentences that best represent the information in the passage.

QUESTION TYPE

Directions: An introductory sentence for a brief summary of the passage is provided below. Complete the summary by selecting the THREE answer choices that express the most important ideas in the passage. Some sentences do not belong in the summary because they express ideas that are not presented in the passage or are minor ideas in the passage.

> Drag your answer choices to the spaces where they belong. To remove an answer choice, click on it. To review the passage, click on **View Text**.

At the beginning of the nineteenth century, Americans were hoping to acquire more land. They were especially interested in Louisiana, which belonged to France, because its Mississippi River provided an important connection for business and trade. Thus, U.S. president Thomas Jefferson sent government officials to France in 1801 in an attempt to purchase New Orleans, the main city of Louisiana. However, 5 French emperor Napoleon rejected their offers at first. France had just won Louisiana from Spain, and Napoleon was planning to establish a western empire in North America. Later on, Jefferson tried to persuade Napoleon to reconsider his offer. This time, since Napoleon needed the money for his war against Britain, he agreed to sell all of Louisiana's territories for 15 million dollars. In 1803, an agreement was reached 10 for the land. Today, the land acquired in the Louisiana Purchase makes up about 23% of U.S. territory.

1 **Directions:** An introductory sentence for a brief summary of the passage is provided below. Complete the summary by selecting the THREE answer choices that express the most important ideas in the passage.

> Before becoming part of the U.S., Louisiana was a territory of France.
> -
> -
> -

Answer Choices

Ⓐ Napoleon had bought Louisiana from Spain to establish an empire in America.

Ⓑ The U.S. earned much money from trade through the Mississippi River.

Ⓒ In 1801, American officials attempted to convince Napoleon to sell Louisiana, but their attempts failed.

Ⓓ France agreed to sell Louisiana to the U.S. to fund their war against Britain.

Ⓔ Around the time of the purchase, the U.S. president was Thomas Jefferson.

Ⓕ Americans wanted to make Louisiana an American territory because of its benefits for business and trade.

BASIC DRILLS 02

Born in Delaware in 1863, Annie Jump Cannon became one of the twentieth century's most remarkable female astronomers. After graduating college with a degree in physics and astronomy, she started to work at the Harvard College Observatory.

At the time, stars were classified according to how much hydrogen they contained. They were assigned letters from A to Q, with A representing stars with the most 5 hydrogen. However, Cannon soon discovered that temperature, not hydrogen content, was the main thing that made stars different from each other. With this information, she reduced the number of classifications and rearranged the remaining letters into the order of O, B, A, F, G, K, M. The hottest stars were classified as O-type and the coolest as M-type. Astronomers accepted Cannon's system, and it became the standard in 10 1922. For the rest of her career, Cannon used her system to classify about 350,000 stars, which were published in a huge list called the Henry Draper Catalogue. Today, astronomers still rely on Cannon's system to classify stars.

1

Directions: An introductory sentence for a brief summary of the passage is provided below. Complete the summary by selecting the THREE answer choices that express the most important ideas in the passage.

> Annie Jump Cannon was a remarkable astronomer of the twentieth century.
> -
> -
> -

Answer Choices

Ⓐ Cannon studied physics and astronomy in college.

Ⓑ Before Cannon's work, stars were grouped according to their hydrogen content.

Ⓒ Cannon discovered a better way of classifying stars: by temperature.

Ⓓ Cannon's system started with the O-type stars and ended with the M-types.

Ⓔ The method that Cannon created was a great contribution to astronomy.

Ⓕ Cannon published the Henry Draper Catalogue to promote her ideas of star classification.

The Invention of Windshield Wipers

 Before the invention of *windshield wipers, drivers used to stop their cars continually and get out to remove the snow and rain from their windshields. However, this changed thanks to a young American inventor named Mary Anderson. She witnessed this 5 inconvenient practice while she was on a trip to New York in the winter of 1902. To solve the inconvenience, she came up with the idea of windshield wipers.

Anderson invented a wiper that consisted of a swinging arm with a rubber blade. It could be controlled by the driver by pulling a handle from the inside of the car. The handle made the arm swing back and forth across the windshield, removing any snow 10 or rain that had accumulated on it. In 1903, she applied for and was given a *patent for this design. Although similar models had been made before Anderson's, hers was the first to work effectively.

➜ At first, the public response to her invention was negative. They laughed at her because they believed the wipers would distract drivers and cause accidents. 15 However, as cars became more popular, windshield wipers became standard equipment. By 1916, all American cars had windshield wipers, and they are still used today.

*windshield: the front window in a car
*patent: the legal right to produce or sell an invention for a certain period of time

1 The word it in the passage refers to
- Ⓐ car
- Ⓑ handle
- Ⓒ arm
- Ⓓ windshield

2   According to paragraph 3, why did people respond negatively to Anderson's invention?

(A) They thought it might lead to accidents.

(B) They did not expect cars to become popular.

(C) They considered the cost of the wipers to be too expensive.

(D) They thought that cleaning windshields by hand was easier.

Paragraph 3 is marked with an arrow [➡].

3   **Directions:** An introductory sentence for a brief summary of the passage is provided below. Complete the summary by selecting the THREE answer choices that express the most important ideas in the passage.

> Mary Anderson invented a piece of equipment that became standard in all cars.
>
> •
>
> •
>
> •

Answer Choices

(A) While traveling in winter, she saw a need for a more efficient way of cleaning car windshields.

(B) Her invention, which she called windshield wipers, was eventually a great success.

(C) Before her design, other windshield wipers had already been made.

(D) Her design included a swinging arm that was operated by a handle.

(E) At one time, people used to have to get out of their cars in order to clean their windshields.

(F) The public was doubtful about her invention at first.

Assemblage Art

Assemblage art is a type of art made from ordinary objects. Anything can be used for assemblages, from a piece of rope to simple junk, such as newspapers and tin cans. The way the objects are put together and displayed may cause viewers to see the objects differently. In this way, assemblages allow artists to explore questions of how people think about or value material things. 5

Assemblage art developed in the early twentieth century as painters and sculptors started incorporating everyday objects in their works. Later on, they began creating assemblages made almost entirely of mass-produced objects and junk, without any original painting elements. Assemblage artists often viewed modern materials in a satirical or critical way. They also began experimenting with three-dimensional 10 assemblages, and some artists even combined performance with the visual arts. These displays appealed to more than just the sense of sight. They represented a new kind of art that people could explore, touch, move, and listen to.

Assemblage art helped change the idea of what art can be. It makes creative connections between distinct materials and gives non-art materials a chance to be a 15 part of an artwork. It also raises questions about what makes something original and who can be an artist. Assemblages also challenge the traditional notion of an artist as a creator, with many assemblage artists never having trained in the arts. Assemblage embraces artists outside the mainstream and has expanded the concepts of both art and the artist. 20

1 The word material in the passage is closest in meaning to

Ⓐ individual   Ⓑ physical

Ⓒ insignificant   Ⓓ antique

2

Which of the sentences below best expresses the essential information in the highlighted sentence in the passage?

Ⓐ More people can be called artists as assemblage art widens the definition of art.

Ⓑ Assemblage artists are not artists according to many art experts' opinions.

Ⓒ Mainstream artists started doing assemblage art to attract non-artists to the art world.

Ⓓ Assemblages are made through the cooperation of both artists and non-artists.

3

Directions: An introductory sentence for a brief summary of the passage is provided below. Complete the summary by selecting the THREE answer choices that express the most important ideas in the passage.

Assemblage is a type of art that makes use of everyday objects.

-
-
-

Answer Choices

Ⓐ Assemblage art started as a movement to acknowledge the value of undervalued objects around us.

Ⓑ Assemblage artists use junk or mass-produced objects for their work.

Ⓒ Assemblage art gives viewers a different perspective on objects and creates new connections between them.

Ⓓ Instead of focusing mainly on our sense of sight, assemblage art focuses more on our other senses.

Ⓔ Many assemblage artists were not able to receive proper training and education.

Ⓕ As an art form, assemblage art changed traditional notions of art and the artist.

The Importance of Rain Forests

Rain forests are forests with tall trees, where temperatures are always warm and rainfall is heavy. About 10% of Earth's land surface is covered by rain forests, but they contain more than half of the world's animal and plant species. Unfortunately, large sections of the forests are cut down each day, and their disappearance has many negative effects. 5

➡ For example, rain forest trees help control the levels of carbon dioxide in the air. Trees get energy by taking in sunlight and carbon dioxide through a process called *photosynthesis. When fewer trees perform photosynthesis, there is more carbon dioxide left in the air. Since it is the main greenhouse gas, increases in carbon dioxide that result from the loss of rain forests speed up global warming. 10

Rain forest trees also keep the soil in the forests from being washed away, as their roots hold the soil in place. However, when the trees are cut down, it becomes easy for heavy rains to wash the soil into rivers. After losing large amounts of soil in this way, the land can no longer support plant life and may eventually become a desert.

Humans benefit from rain forests as well. A quarter of all our medicines come from 15 plants that grow there. Because there are so many plants in the rain forests, we have only been able to study a small number so far. Therefore, the disappearance of rain forests causes many plant species to become extinct before we can even discover them. This means that we may be losing opportunities to develop important new medicines as time goes by. 20

photosynthesis: the process by which green plants turn carbon dioxide and water into food

1 Why does the author discuss carbon dioxide in paragraph 2?
- Ⓐ To identify one of the main greenhouse gases
- Ⓑ To explain how rain forest loss can lead to global problems
- Ⓒ To show an environmental condition of rain forests
- Ⓓ To describe how trees in rain forests perform photosynthesis

Paragraph 2 is marked with an arrow [➡].

2 The word them in the passage refers to

(A) humans

(B) medicines

(C) rain forests

(D) plant species

3 **Directions:** An introductory sentence for a brief summary of the passage is provided below. Complete the summary by selecting the THREE answer choices that express the most important ideas in the passage.

> Since rain forests perform important functions, their loss has many negative effects.
>
> •
>
> •
>
> •

Answer Choices

(A) Most of the medicines we now enjoy originally come from rain forest plants.

(B) The process of photosynthesis carried out by rain forest trees affects carbon dioxide levels.

(C) Rain forests are slowly turning into deserts because soil is continually being washed away by heavy rain.

(D) Rain forests prevent the loss of soil which supports plant life.

(E) Rain forests take up about 10% of Earth's land surface.

(F) The disappearance of rain forests can lead to the loss of potential now medicines.

The Iroquois Longhouse

The Iroquois Indian tribe was a union of six Native American nations. They lived in what is now New York State until the eighteenth century. Although they were commonly known as the Iroquois, they called themselves *Haudenosaunee*. This means "People of the Longhouses." As the name suggests, they lived in long, narrow houses that consisted of one large room.   5

➤ Longhouses were typically from 180 to 220 feet long, but were quite narrow, reaching only 20 feet in width. The frame of the longhouse was made from wood. There were doors on both ends that were usually covered with curtains – made from animal skins – during the cold winters. ■ The skins helped keep the cold out and keep the warmth in. ■ There were no windows, and therefore, darkness filled   10 the interiors of the houses. ■ To keep longhouses warm, fire pits were built on the inside. ■

➤ The purpose of the longhouses was to hold extended families of the same *clan, from 30 to 60 people, or up to 20 families. The families of one longhouse were descended from the same ancestor on the mother's side, and a woman of the   15 clan owned the longhouse. Each family had a personal area inside the longhouse of about six by nine feet. Each of these spaces was separated by leather curtains and contained a wooden platform to sleep on. Clothes and tools were kept beneath the platforms. Baskets, pots, and other items were kept on shelves.

clan: a group of people that can trace their roots to one particular person

TOEFL Reading

1. Why does the author mention *Haudenosaunee*?

   Ⓐ To outline the history of Iroquois Indians

   Ⓑ To explain their relationship with other tribes

   Ⓒ To introduce a major characteristic of Iroquois Indians

   Ⓓ To give a reason why Iroquois Indians lived in New York State

2. According to paragraph 2, why did the Iroquois cover doors with curtains?

   Ⓐ To block out the sun

   Ⓑ To identify the owner of the house

   Ⓒ To make their houses appear unique

   Ⓓ To keep the interiors of their houses warm

   Paragraph 2 is marked with an arrow [➡].

3. Look at the four squares [■] that indicate where the following sentence could be added to the passage.

   Holes were made in the roofs to allow smoke to escape.

   Where would the sentence best fit?

4. What can be inferred from paragraph 3 about Iroquois society?

   Ⓐ It was divided into several social classes.

   Ⓑ Women had a lot of power compared to men.

   Ⓒ It was more developed than other Native American societies.

   Ⓓ Their lifestyle had an influence on other societies.

   Paragraph 3 is marked with an arrow [➡].

5. **Directions:** An introductory sentence for a brief summary of the passage is provided below. Complete the summary by selecting the THREE answer choices that express the most important ideas in the passage. Some sentences do not belong in the summary because they express ideas that are not presented in the passage or are minor ideas in the passage.

The Iroquois Indians were well-known for living in longhouses.

-
-
-

Answer Choices

ⓐ Made from wood, longhouses were long, narrow homes consisting of a single room.

ⓑ The longhouses were bigger than houses used by any other Indian tribe.

ⓒ Longhouses were designed to provide homes for extended families of a clan.

ⓓ Inside a longhouse, each family had an area for personal use.

ⓔ Since longhouses did not have any windows, the inside of the houses was very dark.

ⓕ Protecting each family member's privacy was an essential part of their lives.

Vocabulary Review

A   Choose the correct word for each definition.

> Ⓐ swing   Ⓑ embrace   Ⓒ distract
>
> Ⓓ agreement   Ⓔ extinct   Ⓕ expand

1. no longer existing: _____
2. to move in a curving motion: _____
3. to pull someone's attention away: _____
4. a formal contract between two groups: _____
5. to make something become larger in size, amount, or scope: _____

B   Choose the best synonym for each pair of words.

> Ⓐ item   Ⓑ original   Ⓒ essential
>
> Ⓓ section   Ⓔ acquire   Ⓕ notion

1. concept   idea   : _____
2. thing   object   : _____
3. vital   necessary : _____
4. get   obtain   : _____

C   Fill in the blanks with the best answer.

> degree   platform   operate   potential   inconvenient

1. Max considered the _____ problems and suggested some practical solutions.
2. I went to the University of Toronto and got a(n) _____ in history.
3. On my first day of work, they showed me how to _____ the machines.
4. The location of my apartment is _____ because there's no subway stop nearby.

D Choose the word that is closest in meaning to each highlighted word.

1. His new novel represents his view of life.
   - (A) outlines
   - (B) emphasizes
   - (C) expresses
   - (D) changes

2. Mary purchased a pair of leather boots and a coat.
   - (A) wanted
   - (B) saw
   - (C) bought
   - (D) received

3. The construction workers dug a pit for the foundation.
   - (A) mound
   - (B) place
   - (C) landscape
   - (D) hole

4. All of the items in this bookstore are classified according to genre and author.
   - (A) named
   - (B) priced
   - (C) revised
   - (D) categorized

E Choose the opposite meaning of each highlighted word.

1. I separated my clothes into two piles, one for summer and the other for winter.
   - (A) threw
   - (B) left
   - (C) joined
   - (D) arranged

2. I'm really worried my boss will reject my proposal.
   - (A) accept
   - (B) ignore
   - (C) praise
   - (D) correct

3. Those types of birds commonly build nests on the rocky cliffs.
   - (A) easily
   - (B) rarely
   - (C) especially
   - (D) accurately

F Choose the correct phrase to complete each sentence.

1. She (looked up to / applied for) a scholarship to help pay for college.
2. The speakers at the seminar (consisted of / participated in) five professors.
3. The company would certainly (run across / benefit from) producing a new medicine to treat cancer.

Schematic Table

- Schematic Table questions ask you to put information from the passage into categories.

Sand dunes are hills of sand created by the movement of wind. Depending on how the wind blows in a particular region, sand dunes may take on several different forms, such as a crescent or a star. Crescentic dunes, or barchans are the most common ⁵ type of sand dune. They are shaped like a moon, with two curving arms. Typically, they develop in places where the wind blows from one direction. As the wind continuously blows, it moves the dunes, which can travel as much as 100 meters in a year. Another type of sand dune is the star dune, which is shaped like a starfish. They have three or more arms, which stretch out from a central ¹⁰ hill. These dunes form in places where winds blow from several different directions, often in valleys or near mountain ranges. The effect of such winds causes star dunes to grow in height; some star dunes can reach heights between 200 and 300 meters.

1 **Directions:** Select the appropriate phrases from the answer choices and match them to the type of sand dune to which they relate. TWO of the answer choices will NOT be used.

Answer Choices	Crescentic dunes
Ⓐ May be as tall as 300 meters	▶
Ⓑ Develop where winds blow in the same direction	▶
Ⓒ May move up to 100 meters during a year	**Star dunes**
Ⓓ Usually form near the ocean	
Ⓔ Have three arms or more	▶
Ⓕ Do not generally last for more than a year	▶
Ⓖ May form near mountains or in valleys	▶

BASIC DRILLS 02

There are several differences in how human eyes and dogs' eyes work. Most important among these is their ability to tell the difference between colors. Dogs cannot distinguish between the colors red and green. This is because of a lack of color receivers, called *cones,* in their *retinas. Humans possess three types of *cones,* allowing them to see blue, red, and green; therefore, people can see in full color. In contrast, dogs have a limited range of color vision because they possess just two types of *cones*. Moreover, dogs' eyes are missing another human feature: the *fovea*. This is a region that is responsible for sensing details in an object. Without a *fovea*, dogs cannot recognize the smaller details of something as well as humans can. Finally, night vision is different for humans and dogs. Both humans and dogs possess cells called *rods* that help them to see in dim light, but dogs have more of these cells. Therefore, they can see better in the dark than humans can.

*retina: the area of the eye that receives images from the lens and sends these signals to the brain

1 **Directions:** Select the appropriate phrases from the answer choices and match them to the organism to which they relate. TWO of the answer choices will NOT be used.

Answer Choices	Humans
Ⓐ Do not have a *fovea*	▶
Ⓑ Can distinguish smaller details	▶
Ⓒ Have smaller retinas	
	Dogs
Ⓓ Have three kinds of *cones*	
Ⓔ Cannot see in full color	▶
Ⓕ Have good night vision	▶
Ⓖ Do not have *rods*	▶

Bacteria and Viruses

Bacteria and viruses have been responsible for the deaths of millions of people. Bubonic plague, which is caused by a bacterium, resulted in about 50 million deaths in the fourteenth century. The Spanish flu virus killed at least 50 million people from 1918 to 1919, and coronavirus caused great damage in the early 2020s.

The symptoms of both bacterial and viral infections are similar. They include 5 fatigue, vomiting, inflammation, coughing, sneezing, and fever. These are the immune system's way of trying to drive out infectious organisms from the body. Despite these similarities, however, bacterial and viral infections are different in significant ways. For example, bacteria are usually about 200-1000 nanometers in diameter. Viruses, on the other hand, are much smaller, measuring around 20-400 nanometers in diameter. 10 Additionally, viruses must attach themselves to a host's genetic material in order to survive and multiply. Antibiotics will not work for viral infections. Instead, vaccinations or antiviral drugs must be used to prevent or treat them. Bacteria, on the other hand, can live in a variety of environments and can even be beneficial. Some bacteria are known to protect us from harmful microbes, provide our bodies with nutrients, and aid 15 with digestion. In fact, less than one percent of bacteria cause sickness. When they do, antibiotics can treat the infection. However, it is recommended to let the body's immune system fight off infections alone as overuse of antibiotics can make the body resistant to antibiotic treatments.

1 The word These in the passage refers to
   - Ⓐ bacteria
   - Ⓑ viruses
   - Ⓒ symptoms
   - Ⓓ infections

2 The word beneficial in the passage is closest in meaning to

(A) treatable

(B) essential

(C) considerable

(D) helpful

3 From the passage, it can be inferred that

(A) viruses have killed more people than bacteria have

(B) bacteria have no positive effect on the human body

(C) our body can fight off bacterial infection by itself

(D) most people are naturally resistant to antibiotic treatment

4 **Directions:** Complete the table by matching the phrases below. Select the appropriate phrases from the answer choices and match them to the microorganism to which they relate. TWO of the answer choices will NOT be used.

Answer Choices		Bacteria
(A) Are treatable with antibiotics	▶	
(B) Must attach to a host to survive	▶	
(C) May keep us safe from harmful microorganisms	▶	
(D) Do not produce symptoms		Viruses
(E) Can be prevented with vaccines	▶	
(F) Affect mostly young people	▶	
(G) Help with digestion		

Bees and Wasps

Most people think bees and wasps are very similar, but in reality, they are quite different. Whereas bees possess thick, hairy bodies with flat back legs, wasps have slim bodies with little hair and slender legs shaped like cylinders.   5

When it comes to food, bees spend a lot of time flying between flowers and plants, collecting pollen – a powder-like substance produced by flowers. They gather pollen to nourish their babies. Thanks to their hairy bodies and long legs, they are able to carry this pollen over great distances. Wasps, on the other hand, have a very different diet. They may sometimes eat pollen, but their main   10 sources of food are other insects, spiders, and small dead animals, and they give these to their babies. In order to be better hunters, wasps have slimmer, tighter bodies than bees.

In spite of their differences, both bees and wasps are social insects that live in nests. There, they care for their queen and her babies. But there is a difference here,   15 too. Bees use a wax-like material to build their hives. Wasps, on the other hand, do not have wax-producing organs, so they build their nests out of a paper-like material. They produce this material by chewing wood and other plant remains and adding their *saliva to the mix.

*saliva: a colorless liquid present in the mouth that helps to break down food

1   The word nourish in the passage is closest in meaning to
  Ⓐ feed
  Ⓑ train
  Ⓒ attract
  Ⓓ protect

2 The author mentions wax-producing organs in order to

(A) explain the benefits of bees' nests

(B) describe the difficulty in making wasps' nests

(C) show why wasps' nests are different from bees' nests

(D) compare the physical characteristics of bees to those of wasps

3 According to the passage, which of the following is true about both bees and wasps?

(A) They eat pollen.

(B) They have little hair.

(C) They hunt together in groups.

(D) They produce wax.

4 **Directions:** Complete the table by matching the phrases below. Select the appropriate phrases from the answer choices and match them to the organism to which they relate. TWO of the answer choices will NOT be used.

Answer Choices		Bees
(A) Have wax-producing organs	▶	
(B) Make nests out of chewed plant material	▶	
(C) Use pollen to create their nests		
(D) Have slim bodies that are good for hunting		**Wasps**
(E) Eat insects, spiders, and small dead animals	▶	
(F) Have longer back legs than front legs	▶	
(G) Rely on pollen as their main source of food	▶	

Sleet and Hail

Sleet and hail are both pieces of ice that fall from the sky. Sleet is a small frozen raindrop or snowflake which occurs in winter. In contrast, the round and stone-like hail, occurs at any time of the year, most commonly during thunderstorms.

Sleet and hail form in different ways. Sleet forms when raindrops or melting snowflakes freeze before they reach the ground. This happens when there are warm 5 layers of air high in the atmosphere but cold layers closer to the surface. In the case of raindrops, as they fall from clouds, they meet layers of air at different temperatures. As they approach the ground, the air temperature drops below freezing and the raindrops turn to sleet. As for snowflakes, when they fall through a warm layer, they melt, and then turn into sleet when they pass through a colder layer below. 10

➡ On the other hand, hail forms from raindrops at the bottom of clouds during thunderstorms. Strong wind picks up the raindrops and carries them to the top of thick clouds. There, cold temperatures cause them to freeze. The frozen raindrops start to fall, but the wind sends them up again to the top of the clouds. They undergo the same cycle several times. Each time, the hail collects more water from the bottom of 15 the clouds as it freezes, creating a ball made up of many layers of ice. When these ice balls, or hail stones, become too heavy for the wind to hold up in the air, they finally fall to the ground.

1 The word they in the passage refers to

Ⓐ snowflakes

Ⓑ raindrops

Ⓒ clouds

Ⓓ layers of air

2 The word undergo in the passage is closest in meaning to

   (A) set out

   (B) depend on

   (C) prepare for

   (D) go through

3 According to paragraph 3, hail starts to fall to the ground when

   (A) thunderstorms disappear

   (B) the air temperature is warmer

   (C) the wind cannot support its weight

   (D) the wind suddenly changes direction

Paragraph 3 is marked with an arrow [➡].

4 **Directions:** Complete the table by matching the phrases below. Select the appropriate phrases from the answer choices and match them to the form of precipitation to which they relate. TWO of the answer choices will NOT be used.

Answer Choices	Sleet
(A) Forms during colder months	▶
(B) Forms when warm layers of air are near the ground	▶
(C) Often occurs during thunderstorms	
(D) Changes with air temperature as it falls	**Hail**
(E) Has several ice layers	▶
(F) Requires a longer time to form	▶
(G) Starts to fall several times before reaching the ground	▶

iBT PRACTICE

TOEFL Reading

The Polar Regions

The polar regions refer to the Arctic and the Antarctic, which are located at the northern and southern ends of Earth. ■ Both regions have long, extremely cold winters and short cool summers. ■ They are covered with snow and ice throughout the entire year. ■ Polar regions are also dry, receiving less than 25 centimeters of rainfall and snow each year. ■

5

Despite these similarities, both polar regions have very different characteristics. One key difference is that the Arctic is made up of the mostly frozen Arctic Ocean and the surrounding land–the northern parts of various land masses including the continents of North America, Asia, Europe, and the island of Greenland. In contrast, the Antarctic is a continent surrounded by parts of the Pacific Ocean, the Atlantic Ocean, and the Indian Ocean.

10

The Arctic and the Antarctic are also home to different plant and animal species. The Arctic has rich and varied animal and plant life. It has many *terrestrial animals, such as polar bears, reindeer, and arctic foxes. It also has about 90 flowering plant species. However, the Antarctic, with its colder climate, has few terrestrial animals or trees. Instead, a range of mostly aquatic animals, including whales, penguins, seals, and birds live in the Antarctic.

15

There is yet another difference between the polar regions: the existence of native people. The Arctic is home to various groups of native people. They survive by fishing as well as hunting seals and polar bears. There are some 4 million inhabitants of the Arctic region. However, the Antarctic has no history of any native people. Today, the only people living there are scientists who undertake research on a range of scientific and environmental topics.

20

terrestrial: living on or growing from land, rather than in water or air

TOEFL Reading

1. Look at the four squares [■] that indicate where the following sentence could be
    added to the passage.

       As a result, much of these regions are classified as deserts.

    Where would the sentence best fit?

2. Which of the sentences below best expresses the essential information in the
    highlighted sentence in the passage? *Incorrect* choices change the meaning in
    important ways or leave out essential information.
    (A) The Arctic is located near the northern parts of several continents.
    (B) Composed mainly of frozen water, the Arctic covers very little land.
    (C) The Arctic is mostly frozen ocean and pieces of land from several continents.
    (D) The Arctic actually covers several continents, including North America, Asia,
        Europe, and the island of Greenland.

3. The word inhabitants in the passage is closest in meaning to
    (A) species   (B) residents
    (C) neighbors   (D) communities

4. The word undertake in the passage is closest in meaning to
    (A) plan   (B) conduct
    (C) fund   (D) expect

5. **Directions:** Complete the table by matching the phrases below. Select the appropriate phrases from the answer choices and match them to the polar region to which they relate. TWO of the answer choices will NOT be used.

Answer Choices	The Arctic
Ⓐ Is a continent surrounded by oceans	▶
Ⓑ Is home to reindeer and polar bears	▶
Ⓒ Supports dozens of flowering plant species	
Ⓓ Is one of the wettest regions on Earth	**The Antarctic**
Ⓔ Is a habitat for penguins	▶
Ⓕ Does not have a native population	▶
Ⓖ Has warmer and drier weather	▶

Vocabulary Review

A   Choose the correct word for each definition.

> (A) continuously   (B) distinguish   (C) treatable
>
> (D) protect   (E) diet   (F) infection

1. a disease caused by bacteria or a virus: _____
2. can be cured: _____
3. to recognize a difference: _____
4. without a break or a pause: _____
5. one's everyday food and drink: _____

B   Choose the best synonym for each pair of words.

> (A) existence   (B) region   (C) slender
>
> (D) aid   (E) limited   (F) attach

1. area   section : _____
2. restricted   narrow   : _____
3. help   assist   : _____
4. slim   thin   : _____

C   Fill in the blanks with the best answer.

> resistant   typically   responsible   snowflakes   chewing

1. Large _____ are falling from the sky.
2. Natalie's dog was happily _____ on a bone.
3. The seminar _____ lasts about an hour.
4. The meatballs were _____ for yesterday's food poisoning emergency.

D Choose the word that is closest in meaning to each highlighted word.

1. My son possesses a great talent for drawing.
   - (A) develops
   - (B) has
   - (C) finds
   - (D) hopes

2. Sam will pick you up when you reach your destination.
   - (A) deal with
   - (B) go over
   - (C) get to
   - (D) work on

3. It was difficult to read a book in the dim evening light.
   - (A) late
   - (B) calm
   - (C) faint
   - (D) bright

4. The police found a strange substance at the crime scene.
   - (A) material
   - (B) person
   - (C) problem
   - (D) weapon

E Choose the opposite meaning of each highlighted word.

1. Food with too much trans fat is harmful to our health.
   - (A) beneficial
   - (B) important
   - (C) convenient
   - (D) toxic

2. My ice cream melted fast because of the hot weather.
   - (A) disappeared
   - (B) improved
   - (C) changed
   - (D) froze

3. The commander punished her soldiers for their lack of seriousness.
   - (A) praise
   - (B) quantity
   - (C) excess
   - (D) control

F Choose the correct phrase to complete each sentence.

1. This type of plastic has (in spite of / a range of) uses.
2. The store sells furniture (as well as / in contrast to) home appliances.
3. The leader seems confident, but (what is more / in reality) the plan is almost impossible to carry out.

Actual Practice Test

ACTUAL PRACTICE TEST 3

Ocean Zones

Far from shore, the ocean is very deep. To understand it better, scientists have divided it into three zones according to the amount of sunlight received. Each zone has a different environment that sustains different kinds of life.

The first zone includes the ocean surface and extends down to a depth of about 200 meters. Because it is so close to the surface, it receives abundant sunlight and is therefore known as the sunlight zone. Its warm temperatures and sunny waters are ideal for a variety of creatures, so the sunlight zone is filled with life. There are tiny plankton, fish of all shapes and sizes, and some of the largest mammals on Earth. All of them depend on the plant life in the sunlight zone for their survival. The sunlight zone is the only zone where there is enough sunlight for plants to perform photosynthesis.

→ Beneath the sunlight zone, between depths of about 200 to 1,000 meters, lies a darker region of water called the twilight zone. ■ It receives very little sunlight. ■ The lack of sunlight makes photosynthesis impossible, so there is no plant life. ■ The absence of plant life leaves residents of the twilight zone with few sources of food. ■ In spite of this, the twilight zone is not empty of life. Animals like squid, eels, and octopuses live in the dark water. These creatures mainly feed on plant matter and particles of waste that float down from the sunlight zone, though, at times, some may travel upward to find food in the rich zone above.

→ The deepest zone of the ocean is known as the midnight zone. It covers the depths between 1,000 meters and the ocean floor. It is an extreme environment, where the temperature is near freezing, the pressure is great, and there is absolutely no light. Few animals are able to endure the conditions of the midnight zone, yet life exists there nonetheless. The anglerfish and the giant squid can be found in the deepest parts of the ocean. As in the twilight zone, life in the midnight zone depends on tiny pieces of waste that sink down from above.

1. The author mentions the amount of sunlight in order to

    Ⓐ introduce the division of the ocean into zones

    Ⓑ suggest that there is little plant life in the ocean

    Ⓒ describe the effect of sunlight on life in the ocean

    Ⓓ explain the main difference between ocean and land environments

2. The word sustains in the passage is closest in meaning to

    Ⓐ causes   Ⓑ favors

    Ⓒ protects   Ⓓ supports

3. The word it in the passage refers to

    Ⓐ shore   Ⓑ depth

    Ⓒ ocean surface   Ⓓ sunlight zone

4. Which of the sentences below best expresses the essential information in the highlighted sentence in the passage? *Incorrect* choices change the meaning in important ways or leave out essential information.

    Ⓐ Creatures living in the twilight zone leave their home when food is scarce.

    Ⓑ Since plants cannot exist in the twilight zone, it is hard for residents of the zone to survive.

    Ⓒ Creatures in the twilight zone do not have enough food as there are no plants growing there.

    Ⓓ Animals living in the twilight zone do not feed on plants.

5. According to paragraph 3, what kind of food do animals in the twilight zone live on?

   Ⓐ Plankton and small fish

   Ⓑ Squid, eels, and octopuses

   Ⓒ Waste that sinks down from the zone above

   Ⓓ Plant species that grow on the ocean floor

Paragraph 3 is marked with an arrow [➝].

6. The word endure in the passage is closest in meaning to

   Ⓐ stand   Ⓑ recover

   Ⓒ resist   Ⓓ change

7. All of the following are mentioned in paragraph 4 as characteristics that make the midnight zone a difficult environment to live in EXCEPT

   Ⓐ the absence of sunlight

   Ⓑ the high water pressure

   Ⓒ the very cold temperature

   Ⓓ the existence of meat-eating animals

Paragraph 4 is marked with an arrow [➝].

8. In what order does the author explain the zones of the ocean?

   Ⓐ From the surface to the bottom

   Ⓑ From the largest to the smallest

   Ⓒ From the coolest to the warmest

   Ⓓ From the least familiar to the most familiar

9. Look at the four squares [■] that indicate where the following sentence could be added to the passage.

> Therefore, the water is much colder, with temperatures reaching as low as 4°C.

Where would the sentence best fit?

Click on a square [■] to add the sentence to the passage.

10. **Directions:** Complete the table by matching the phrases below. Select the appropriate phrases from the answer choices and match them to the ocean zone to which they relate. TWO of the answer choices will NOT be used.

Drag your answer choices to the spaces where they belong. To remove an answer choice, click on it. To review the passage, click on **View Text**.

Answer Choices	Sunlight zone
(A) Contains plants that perform photosynthesis	▶
(B) Is the most extreme ocean environment	▶
(C) Is warmer than the other zones	▶
(D) Is unable to support any form of life	**Twilight zone**
(E) Covers depths from 200 to 1,000 meters	
(F) Is home to species like the giant squid	▶
(G) Is the largest environment on Earth	▶
(H) Supports some of the largest mammals on Earth	**Midnight zone**
(I) Contains animals that move to another zone for food	▶
	▶

ACTUAL PRACTICE TEST 3

Wangari Maathai

→ Wangari Maathai was an environmental and political activist who was born in Kenya in 1940. Though rare for girls at the time, her family sent her off to school, where she excelled. She went to the United States in 1960 to study biology and went on to receive her master's degree in biological sciences. During this time, she witnessed the American civil rights and anti-Vietnam War movements and was inspired by them.

→ Upon returning to Kenya, Maathai attended the University of Nairobi to study veterinary anatomy. She became the first woman in East Africa to obtain a doctorate degree and also became the first woman in the region to be the chair of a university department. At about this time, Maathai began her new mission to safeguard Kenya's natural lands and resources that had been negatively affected by development. She did this by starting the Green Belt Movement in 1977. She encouraged the nation's women to plant trees throughout the country and helped them to receive a stipend. The movement was so effective that it is credited with adding 30 million trees in Kenya and supplying new skills and job opportunities to 30,000 women.

As a result of challenging the government on its development plans for the country, Maathai endured physical abuse and multiple imprisonments. ■ Her most well-known act was a protest held in 1989 at Nairobi's Uhuru Park to stop a skyscraper's construction. ■ It also resulted in the imprisonment of many protesters, whom Maathai fought to release. ■ This struggle helped her to realize that Kenya's underlying problem was poor governance. ■

In 2004, she finally won the Nobel Peace Prize for her contribution to human rights, women's rights, and democracy in her push for sustainable development. Maathai said in her Nobel speech that peace was only possible with equitable development and sustainable management of the environment in a democratic nation. To many she represented how one person with enough persistence can

leave a positive mark on the world.

Glossary
stipend: an amount of money paid regularly to someone

11. What can be inferred from paragraph 1 about American society in the 1960s?

   Ⓐ It was rare for girls to receive a proper education.

   Ⓑ Many students from Africa studied in the U.S.

   Ⓒ Demonstrations against the Vietnam War were actively held.

   Ⓓ University research supported industries important to the Vietnam War.

   Paragraph 1 is marked with an arrow [➡].

12. The word obtain in the passage is closest in meaning to

   Ⓐ define   Ⓑ earn   Ⓒ allow   Ⓓ improve

13. Which of the sentences below best expresses the essential information in the highlighted sentence in the passage? *Incorrect* choices change the meaning in important ways or leave out essential information.

   Ⓐ Kenya's lands and resources had been harmed because of indiscriminate development at that time.

   Ⓑ Maathai started seeking ways of using Kenya's lands and resources efficiently to help her country become more developed.

   Ⓒ To protect Kenya's damaged land and resources from development, Maathai took on the responsibility of conserving them.

   Ⓓ Maathai recognized the negative effect of development on her country's lands and resources as Kenya grew more and more economically powerful.

14. The word it in the passage refers to

   Ⓐ development   Ⓑ movement   Ⓒ country   Ⓓ stipend

15. According to paragraph 2, it can be inferred that

    Ⓐ Maathai was the first woman to become a medical doctor in Kenya

    Ⓑ the Kenyan government was prevented from cutting down trees

    Ⓒ women in Kenya donated money to support Maathai's Green Belt Movement

    Ⓓ Maathai contributed to protecting women's rights and Kenya's environment

Paragraph 2 is marked with an arrow [➡].

16. The author mentions physical abuse and multiple imprisonments in order to

    Ⓐ emphasize Maathai's commitment to her beliefs

    Ⓑ describe what prevented her from succeeding

    Ⓒ illustrate the problem of women worker's rights

    Ⓓ provide details about Maathai's prison life

17. The word equitable in the passage is closest in meaning to

    Ⓐ essential   Ⓑ standard   Ⓒ complete   Ⓓ fair

18. All of the following are mentioned as achievements of Maathai EXCEPT

    Ⓐ she studied biological science for her master's degree

    Ⓑ she was the first woman to chair a university department in Kenya

    Ⓒ she prevented the government from putting protesters in prison

    Ⓓ she received the Nobel Peace Prize for her work

19. Look at the four squares [■] that indicate where the following sentence could be added to the passage.

    The protest gained global attention and the builders finally ceased construction.

Where would the sentence best fit?

Click on a square [■] to add the sentence to the passage.

20. **Directions:** An introductory sentence for a brief summary of the passage is provided below. Complete the summary by selecting the THREE answer choices that express the most important ideas in the passage. Some sentences do not belong in the summary because they express ideas that are not presented in the passage or are minor ideas in the passage.

> Wangari Maathai is considered a great twentieth-century humanitarian and activist from Kenya.
>
> •
>
> •
>
> •

Answer Choices

(A) Maathai majored in biological science and veterinary anatomy and had an interest in helping people in need.

(B) While Maathai was very successful in her academic career, she wanted to be involved in political activism in her home country.

(C) Maathai witnessed American civil rights and anti-Vietnam War movements when she studied in America.

(D) By setting up the Green Belt Movement, Maathai successfully helped women get jobs and added 30 million trees to Kenya.

(E) Though she was punished for resisting development policies, she eventually became a political leader.

(F) Maathai was recognized for her dedication to the environment and human rights and awarded the Nobel Peace Prize in 2004.

Drag your answer choices to the spaces where they belong. To remove an answer choice, click on it. To review the passage, click on **View Text**.

Answer Keys

UNIT 01 Vocabulary

BASIC DRILLS pp.10~11

| 01 | 1. Ⓑ | 2. Ⓒ | 3. Ⓓ |
| 02 | 1. Ⓐ | 2. Ⓑ | 3. Ⓒ |

READING PRACTICE pp.12~17

01 1. Ⓓ 2. Ⓒ 3. 2nd 4. Ⓒ
Organization
mammals, fur, round, backwards, underground

02 1. Ⓒ 2. Ⓓ 3. Ⓐ 4. Ⓒ
Summary
weather, small, chaos, unpredictable, single

03 1. Ⓑ 2. Ⓑ 3. Ⓒ 4. Ⓓ
Organization
London, pickle, middle, gaps, sunlight, heat

iBT PRACTICE pp.18~20

| 1. Ⓐ | 2. Ⓐ | 3. Ⓒ | 4. Ⓑ | 5. Ⓑ, Ⓒ, Ⓕ |

VOCABULARY REVIEW pp.21~22

A	1. Ⓔ	2. Ⓕ	3. Ⓑ	4. Ⓐ	5. Ⓓ
B	1. Ⓑ	2. Ⓒ	3. Ⓓ	4. Ⓕ	
C	1. lower 2. details 3. unpredictable
	4. temperature
D	1. Ⓒ	2. Ⓓ	3. Ⓐ	4. Ⓑ	
E	1. Ⓐ	2. Ⓓ	3. Ⓓ		
F	1. number in 2. as a result of
	3. have an influence on

UNIT 02 Reference

BASIC DRILLS pp.24~25

| 01 | 1. Ⓒ | 2. Ⓑ |
| 02 | 1. Ⓑ | 2. Ⓒ |

READING PRACTICE pp.26~31

01 1. Ⓒ 2. Ⓑ 3. Ⓒ 4. Ⓓ
Summary
wooden, fire, winds, homeless, buildings

02 1. Ⓓ 2. Ⓒ 3. Ⓑ, Ⓒ, Ⓔ
Organization
upset, seven, recognize, return

03 1. Ⓓ 2. Ⓑ 3. Ⓒ 4. Ⓓ
Summary
lake, earthquake, ice dams, Global warming,
glaciers

iBT PRACTICE pp.32~34

| 1. Ⓓ | 2. Ⓓ | 3. Ⓒ | 4. Ⓑ | 5. Ⓒ | 6. Ⓐ |

VOCABULARY REVIEW pp.35~36

A	1. Ⓔ	2. Ⓐ	3. Ⓕ	4. Ⓓ	5. Ⓒ
B	1. Ⓐ	2. Ⓔ	3. Ⓓ	4. Ⓑ	
C	1. harvest 2. melt 3. digest
	4. phenomenon
D	1. Ⓒ	2. Ⓑ	3. Ⓑ	4. Ⓓ	
E	1. Ⓒ	2. Ⓐ	3. Ⓐ		
F	1. go through 2. put out 3. break up

UNIT 03 Fact & Negative Fact

BASIC DRILLS

pp.38~39

| 01 | 1. B | 2. A |
| 02 | 1. B | 2. A |

READING PRACTICE

pp.40~45

01 1. A 2. C 3. A 4. B

Summary

George Washington, tallest, competition, Civil War, 1884

02 1. D 2. C 3. D 4. D

Organization

three, curved, compound, longer, wood

03 1. A 2. A 3. C 4. D

Organization

Harappan, bricks, roads, mystery

iBT PRACTICE

pp.46~48

1. B 2. A 3. C 4. C 5. B, E, F

VOCABULARY REVIEW

pp.49~50

A 1. E 2. A 3. F 4. D 5. B
B 1. A 2. E 3. D 4. F
C 1. roughly 2. advanced 3. architect
   4. judges
D 1. A 2. B 3. D 4. D
E 1. B 2. C 3. A
F 1. In contrast to 2. made up of
   3. named after

UNIT 04 Sentence Simplification

BASIC DRILLS

pp.52~53

| 01 | 1. B | 2. D |
| 02 | 1. C | 2. D |

READING PRACTICE

pp.54~59

01 1. A 2. D 3. C 4. B

Organization

climate, proxies, snow, fossils

02 1. D 2. C 3. A 4. B

Summary

ocean, air pressure, documentaries, ecosystems

03 1. A 2. B 3. B 4. D

Organization

engines, backwards, gravity, straight, strongest

iBT PRACTICE

pp.60~62

1. D 2. C 3. C 4. A 5. B, C, F

VOCABULARY REVIEW

pp.63~64

A 1. B 2. E 3. A 4. C 5. F
B 1. B 2. E 3. F 4. D
C 1. saltiness 2. independence 3. breathe
   4. encouraged
D 1. C 2. A 3. B 4. B
E 1. C 2. D 3. A
F 1. pumped into 2. involved in
   3. going about

Actual Practice Test 1

1. D   2. B   3. B   4. C   5. A   6. C
7. B   8. A   9. 3rd   10. Epidermis layer: F
/ Dermis layer: B , D / Subcutaneous layer:
A , E

UNIT 05 Inference

BASIC DRILLS   pp.72~73

01 1. D   2. B
02 1. C   2. D

READING PRACTICE   pp.74~79

01 1. 1st   2. C   3. B   4. C
Summary
slavery, Underground Railroad, escape,
transportation, 100,000

02 1. A   2. C   3. D   4. C
Organization
beetle, humid, streams, light, predators

03 1. C   2. B   3. 2nd   4. C
Summary
Africa, upright, skulls, tools, fire

iBT PRACTICE   pp.80~82

1. C   2. D   3. A   4. A   5. A , C , F

VOCABULARY REVIEW   pp.83~84

A 1. A   2. F   3. D   4. B   5. C
B 1. A   2. B   3. F   4. D
C 1. ax   2. appeared   3. chemicals   4. driven

D 1. C   2. A   3. D   4. B
E 1. A   2. B   3. D
F 1. participated in   2. get used to
   3. is responsible for

UNIT 06 Rhetorical Purpose

BASIC DRILLS   pp.86~87

01 1. C   2. D
02 1. B   2. D

READING PRACTICE   pp.88~93

01 1. A   2. C   3. A   4. D
Summary
nature, birds, catalog, *Birds of America*

02 1. D   2. C   3. C   4. C
Summary
volcano, earthquake, ash, animals

03 1. A   2. B   3. D   4. C
Organization
causes, external, internal, external, succeed, fail

iBT PRACTICE   pp.94~96

1. B   2. D   3. A   4. D   5. B , D , E

VOCABULARY REVIEW   pp.97~98

A 1. B   2. F   3. D   4. C   5. E
B 1. C   2. E   3. F   4. A
C 1. yelled   2. earthquake   3. judgment
   4. combine
D 1. B   2. C   3. C   4. A
E 1. C   2. D   3. D
F 1. piled up   2. slide down   3. related to

E 1. Ⓑ 2. Ⓑ 3. Ⓐ
F 1. ahead of 2. linked to 3. depending on

Actual Practice Test

pp.100~103

1. Ⓐ 2. Ⓒ 3. Ⓐ 4. Ⓓ 5. Ⓑ 6. Ⓓ
7. Ⓒ 8. Ⓐ 9. 4th 10. Athens: Ⓐ, Ⓒ,
Ⓕ / Sparta: Ⓓ, Ⓔ

UNIT 07 Insertion

BASIC DRILLS

pp.106~107

01 1. 1B 2. 2C
02 1. 1D 2. 2A

READING PRACTICE

pp.108~113

01 1. Ⓓ 2. 3rd 3. 3rd 4. Ⓒ
Summary
four, hunts, fight, sponsor

02 1. Ⓐ 2. 3rd 3. 2nd 4. Ⓒ
Summary
dangerous, colored, electricity, yellow

03 1. 2nd 2. 2nd 3. Ⓐ 4. Ⓓ
Organization
lines, equator, positive, negative, vertically, 180

iBT PRACTICE

pp.114~116

1. Ⓓ 2. Ⓒ 3. Ⓑ 4. 3rd 5. Ⓐ, Ⓒ, Ⓔ

VOCABULARY REVIEW

pp.117~118

A 1. Ⓕ 2. Ⓐ 3. Ⓔ 4. Ⓑ 5. Ⓒ
B 1. Ⓓ 2. Ⓔ 3. Ⓒ 4. Ⓑ
C 1. composition 2. chaotic 3. distinguish
4. imaginary
D 1. Ⓐ 2. Ⓒ 3. Ⓑ 4. Ⓓ

UNIT 08 Prose Summary

BASIC DRILLS

pp.120~121

01 1. Ⓒ, Ⓓ, Ⓕ
02 1. Ⓑ, Ⓒ, Ⓔ

READING PRACTICE

pp.122~127

01 1. Ⓓ 2. Ⓐ 3. Ⓐ, Ⓑ, Ⓓ
02 1. Ⓑ 2. Ⓐ 3. Ⓑ, Ⓒ, Ⓕ
03 1. Ⓑ 2. Ⓓ 3. Ⓑ, Ⓓ, Ⓕ

iBT PRACTICE

pp.128~130

1. Ⓒ 2. Ⓓ 3. 4th 4. Ⓑ 5. Ⓐ, Ⓒ, Ⓓ

VOCABULARY REVIEW

pp.131~132

A 1. Ⓔ 2. Ⓐ 3. Ⓒ 4. Ⓓ 5. Ⓕ
B 1. Ⓕ 2. Ⓐ 3. Ⓒ 4. Ⓔ
C 1. potential 2. degree 3. operate
4. inconvenient
D 1. Ⓒ 2. Ⓒ 3. Ⓓ 4. Ⓓ
E 1. Ⓒ 2. Ⓐ 3. Ⓑ
F 1. applied for 2. consisted of
3. benefit from

UNIT 09 Schematic Table

Actual Practice Test 3

pp.148~155

1. Ⓐ	2. Ⓓ	3. Ⓓ

1. Ⓐ   2. Ⓓ   3. Ⓓ   4. Ⓒ   5. Ⓒ   6. Ⓐ
7. Ⓓ   8. Ⓐ   9. 2nd   10. Sunlight zone: Ⓐ,
Ⓒ, Ⓗ / Twilight zone: Ⓔ, Ⓘ / Midnight zone:
Ⓑ, Ⓕ   11. Ⓒ   12. Ⓑ   13. Ⓒ   14. Ⓑ
15. Ⓓ   16. Ⓐ   17. Ⓓ   18. Ⓒ   19. 2nd
20. Ⓑ, Ⓓ, Ⓕ

BASIC DRILLS

pp.134~135

01 1. Crescentic dunes: Ⓑ, Ⓒ /
Star dunes: Ⓐ, Ⓔ, Ⓖ
02 1. Humans: Ⓑ, Ⓓ /
Dogs: Ⓐ, Ⓔ, Ⓕ

READING PRACTICE

pp.136~141

01 1. Ⓒ   2. Ⓓ   3. Ⓒ   4. Bacteria: Ⓐ,
Ⓒ, Ⓖ / Viruses: Ⓑ, Ⓔ
02 1. Ⓐ   2. Ⓒ   3. Ⓐ   4. Bees: Ⓐ, Ⓖ /
Wasps: Ⓑ, Ⓓ, Ⓔ
03 1. Ⓑ   2. Ⓓ   3. Ⓒ   4. Sleet: Ⓐ, Ⓓ /
Hail: Ⓒ, Ⓔ, Ⓖ

iBT PRACTICE

pp.142~144

1. 4th   2. Ⓒ   3. Ⓑ   4. Ⓑ   5. The Arctic:
Ⓑ, Ⓒ / The Antarctic: Ⓐ, Ⓔ, Ⓕ

VOCABULARY REVIEW

pp.145~146

A 1. Ⓕ   2. Ⓒ   3. Ⓑ   4. Ⓐ   5. Ⓔ
B 1. Ⓑ   2. Ⓔ   3. Ⓓ   4. Ⓒ
C 1. snowflakes   2. chewing   3. typically
4. responsible
D 1. Ⓑ   2. Ⓒ   3. Ⓒ   4. Ⓐ
E 1. Ⓐ   2. Ⓓ   3. Ⓒ
F 1. a range of   2. as well as   3. in reality